Also available from the
8 Keys to Mental Health Series

8 Keys to Mental Health Series
Babette Rothschild, Series Editor

The 8 Keys series of books provides readers with brief, inexpensive, and high-quality self-help books on a variety of topics in mental health. Each volume is written by an expert in the field, someone who is capable of presenting evidence-based information in a concise and clear way. These books stand out by offering consumers cutting-edge, relevant theory in easily digestible portions, written in an accessible style. The tone is respectful of the reader and the messages are immediately applicable. Filled with exercises and practical strategies, these books empower readers to help themselves.

8 KEYS TO FORGIVENESS

ROBERT ENRIGHT

FOREWORD BY BABETTE ROTHSCHILD

W. W. Norton & Company
New York • London

For information about permission to reproduce selections from this book, write to
Permissions, W. W. Norton & Company, Inc., 500 Fifth Avenue, New York, NY 10110

For information about special discounts for bulk purchases, please contact W. W. Norton
Special Sales at specialsales@wwnorton.com or 800-233-4830

Manufacturing by RR Donnelley Harrisonburg
Production manager: Christine Critelli

Library of Congress Cataloging-in-Publication Data
Enright, Robert D.
8 keys to forgiveness / Robert Enright ; foreword by Babette Rothschild.
pages cm. — (8 keys to mental health series)
Includes bibliographical references and index.
ISBN 978-0-393-73405-8 (pbk.)
1. Forgiveness. I. Title. II. Title: Eight keys to forgiveness.
BF637.F67E567 2015
158.2—dc23
2015017866

W. W. Norton & Company, Inc., 500 Fifth Avenue, New York, N.Y. 10110
www.wwnorton.com

W. W. Norton & Company Ltd., Castle House, 75/76 Wells Street, London W1T 3QT

1 2 3 4 5 6 7 8 9 0

*To Thomas Walker of Mid-West Family Broadcasting
and the entire Walker family for supporting the forgiveness
work at the International Forgiveness Institute, Inc., and
the University of Wisconsin-Madison for decades.
Your persistence, vision, and unwavering support
are astounding. Thank you.*

Contents

Acknowledgments

The 8 *Keys to Forgiveness* is a team effort. Thank you, Babette Rothschild, for inviting me to be a part of this intriguing series. Thank you to the talented editorial staff at W. W. Norton: Andrea Costella Dawson, Benjamin Yarling, Margaret Ryan, and Kathryn Moyer. You have helped me to think more deeply about my chosen life's topic of forgiveness. Jacqueline Song, your reading and discussing the manuscript with me has been invaluable. You have clarified my thinking. Dennis Blang, Director of the International Forgiveness Institute, Inc., you have done so much to advance the presence of forgiveness in the world and for that I am deeply grateful. The academic climate at the University of Wisconsin-Madison has been fertile ground which helped to bring forth the social scientific study of forgiveness. To my wonderful family, thank you for your great support: Shawn, Anna, Peter, Joseph, Kevin, Maria, and Jerome.

Foreword

Babette Rothschild, Series Editor

When I share my woes with one of my dear friends, who also happens to be a Buddhist, she is usually very quick to ask me, "Have you forgiven . . ." whomever it is I am irked by or complaining about. To be honest, I sometimes find this irritating. It's not that I am against forgiveness in principle. It is just that before I can forgive someone, I usually need to feel how angry, upset, disappointed, or hurt I am and have been. And, truth be told, I want to reserve the right to *not* forgive someone if that is my choice. However, I have to admit that this forgiving friend of mine is much more carefree than I am. She seems less bothered by behaviors that I might find irritating or insulting. She sleeps deeper and longer than I do. So I have to wonder, is she on to something in being so quick to forgive transgressors?

The tenth edition of *Merriam-Webster's Collegiate Dictionary* defines "forgiving" as, "allowing room for error or weakness," and "to forgive" as, "to cease to feel resentment." Critical to Enright's approach is a clear distinction between forgiving and condoning or forgetting whatever injury has been done. He asserts, and I agree, that those are not at all the same thing. Forgiveness recognizes human frailty, that everyone can (and does) hurt others. But that in no way condones or excuses the hurting. And it does not free the perpetrator of responsibility for his or her actions or any owed reparation.

The benefit of forgiveness is often more for the one who is hurt. Resentment and bitterness exact a cost on the body and mind that can actually do further harm. This is why Enright will argue that forgiveness could save your life. A mind free of resentment and bitterness is more peaceful, and the body therefore less stressed. Reducing stress, as we all know, is healthy for our blood pressure, hearts, immune systems, and more. So, more than anything, forgiveness is, indeed, much more for your own health than for the benefit of the other.

You have probably chosen this book because you have one or more forgiveness dilemmas in your life. Someone or someones have hurt you, and you have not only suffered from that hurt but are continuing to suffer, because you don't know whether or not to forgive the one or ones who have hurt you. Your mind may be preoccupied with these dilemmas. Or you may revisit them on a regular basis. You wonder if forgiving will free the offender of responsibility, or if you will feel better or worse by giving forgiveness. Or, perhaps, you are the one who has offended against another and you want to ask for forgiveness, either from the one you hurt or from yourself. All of these situations are painful predicaments. This book will give you new ways of thinking about them as well as many tools for making these kinds of difficult decisions, both now and in the future.

The approach of this book is not a religious one. There are a plethora of religious books that address forgiveness. What is offered among these pages is a nonsectarian view of the benefits of forgiveness for everyone, regardless of religion or culture. Like most things in life, whether or not to forgive is generally a personal decision made on a case-by-case basis. Everyone struggles with it at one or more times. Is it a question of morality? Of spirituality? Of mental health? Of humanity? What are the consequences—benefits and risks—when we choose to forgive and when we do not? Enright addresses these topics and more. Accessibly written, readers will find his information and his exercises to be useful in addressing issues of forgiveness, specifically and in general.

Forgiveness is a hot topic on the internet. A web search reveals thousands of websites on the topic. Many are of a religious nature. Others are not based on religion. There are a multitude of sub-themes within each type, addressing specific questions such as:

How do I forgive my husband for lying?

How do I forgive myself for past mistakes?

How do I forgive someone who continues to hurt me?

How do I forgive a cheating boyfriend?

How do I forgive child abuse?

. . . and so on . . .

The long and the short of it is that people not only suffer from the hurts done to them but also from the aftermath of those hurts. Those searching the internet for answers to these questions are examples of individuals suffering not only from being hurt but also from their inability or reluctance to forgive.

But what of the question, "To forgive or not to forgive?" Simon Wiesenthal, a concentration camp survivor who is well known for his work as a Nazi Hunter in the wake of World War II poses this very question in his famous book, *The Sunflower: On the Possibilities and Limits of Forgiveness* (1969). In *The Sunflower* Wiesenthal recounts personal events during the Holo-caust that caused him to question the role of forgiveness in human relationships. As a prisoner in a concentration camp he had a singular experience when he was called to the bedside of a dying SS officer, a Nazi, while on a work detail at a nearby hospital. A nurse had to sneak him into the Nazi's room because the hospital was not a place where Jews of the neighboring camp were allowed. The room was more a death chamber; there was no doubt that the Nazi had little time left. It was a strange turn of events for the prisoner. Stranger still was the wish of the dying officer for Wiesenthal to be his confessor, to recount to him the worst that he had done. And, eventually, to beg Weisenthal to grant him forgiveness for his horrendous Nazi crimes. The officer wished to "die in peace" but his conscience was too troubled to be able to do so.

Wiesenthal suffered under the weight of the request and left the Nazi's room without giving him his forgiveness. But his decision was not straightforward. The request haunted him while awake and in his dreams. He discussed the situation with his closest friends in the camp, but they could not relate to his conflict. They were sure he had done the right thing, that he should not have forgiven the SS officer, that to do so would have been wrong.

Miraculously, Wiesenthal continued to survive despite disease and starvation. His closest friends did not. Before he was liberated, he spent some time with a fellow prisoner who was to become a priest. This young man was not as sure of the answer to the question of forgiveness as Wiesenthal's friends had been. The would-be priest considered forgiveness something you gave to someone who had wronged you personally, that you couldn't forgive wrong done to someone else. However, he also considered that the Nazi was not able to ask forgiveness of those he had murdered, and so had sought Wiesenthal as a sort of representative. The nearly priest was convinced that the Nazi had shown signs of genuine remorse and so his opinion was that forgiveness had been warranted.

At the end of this mini-memoir, Wisenthal questions whether his withholding of forgiveness had been the right thing to do. It is a question that continued to perplex him. And he asks his reader to ask himself, "What would I have done?" He then poses the same question to prominent people, including the Dalai Lama. The rest of the book is comprised of their many and varied responses. I invite you to consider how you would answer this question now, before reading *this* book. And then revisit the question after completing it.

Through these pages, Enright will help you to clarify why forgiveness matters in your life and how it may benefit you to become a more forgiving person. He will provide you with hard data on the advantages of forgiveness for your emotional and physical health. He will provide you with strategies for dealing with difficult forgiveness dilemmas. And, to my mind most importantly, he will help you to, first and foremost, forgive yourself.

KEY 1

KNOW WHY FORGIVENESS MATTERS AND WHAT IT IS

Forgiveness is a quiet gift that you leave on the doorstep of those who have hurt you. Some never open the door to receive it, but for those who do, you are giving them a second chance at a beautiful life. As you forgive, you are giving yourself a second chance at that beautiful life regardless of the other's decision.

Forgiveness can save your life. None of us wants to waste time when it comes to our own healing. It is better to get right to the kind of medicine that will be helpful. I surely would not have spent the last 30 years studying the topic of forgiveness if I were not convinced that forgiveness matters. Sometimes life hits us so hard that our options narrow when it comes to finding healing for the blow. I have never found anything as effective as forgiveness for healing deep wounds. Forgiveness is strong medicine. The purpose of this chapter is to share this insight with you so that you are ready to use the other seven keys with confidence that you are taking a path that is right for your own well-being.

A Case Study to Show Why and How Forgiveness Matters

His bags were not yet packed. Kenneth was offered his dream job in another part of the country, but he could not find a way to leave. He was depressed, discouraged. His relationship with his mother,

Carmen, was nonexistent because of the constant and harsh criticism he had endured from her when he was a child. Recently, Carmen had made an attempt at reconciliation with Kenneth, now that he was grown and she no longer felt pressured to parent him. Just the thought of meeting with his mother enraged Kenneth, however. He was exhausted. "I will not meet with her now—she robbed me of my childhood," Kenneth contended. He felt utterly defeated and yet, deep down, he began to blame himself for all of the conflict. "What did I do wrong? What could I have done differently?" he wondered, over and over. The accusations swirled around in his head, and so he could not pack to leave because he did not have the energy or the focus.

Guess whom he started to dislike the most—*himself.* As he began his internal dialogue, Kenneth became his own harsh critic of himself. His inner dialogue always spiraled back to *his* inadequacies, *his* failures, *his* seeming inability to be loved. He just did not like who he was.

You may or may not relate to the particulars of Kenneth's experience, but it's likely that you've heard your own share of self-accusatory rumblings—those thoughts that come and go in your mind, carrying messages of your failures and wrongdoings. Self-criticism seems part and parcel of the human experience. If we are not careful, however, these critical inner dialogues can and do become a part of us, hurting us sometimes even more than the original injustices did. Under these circumstances, the injustice wins twice: once in its hurtful actions and a second time by its effects dominating every aspect of our lives.

Kenneth stated early in therapy that he would never forgive his mother for her ruthless criticisms years ago. It was just too much. Kenneth's announcement that he would never forgive his mother was not said in defiance of the forgiveness therapy itself. He was just giving a friendly warning that the therapy would not work. He was saying this more for the therapist's sake than for his, so that the therapist would not feel badly when the treatment failed.

Despite this initial pessimism about it, Kenneth proceeded to examine forgiveness, as we will begin to do in this chapter, and to take the other keys and enter the other doors of forgiveness. At the end of his therapy, he not only forgave his mother but also agreed to meet with her to hear what his mother had to say, and he reminded himself that he would listen with a genuine and open mind. His depression, which was considerable at the beginning of the sessions, went away. Sometimes depression can be cyclical, coming and going, but in his case the depression was still absent four months after the therapy ended.

Having a greater appreciation of himself and a renewed energy and enthusiasm for life, Kenneth *did* pack his bags and leave his hometown to pursue his dream job. He was healed of the effects of his mother's harsh ways so many years ago now. Kenneth got his life back.

Forgiveness matters primarily because it can reverse all of the lies you might believe about yourself. You are *not* defeated by others' unjust actions. You *can* overcome discouragement. You *can* stop the inner dialogue of accusation and judgment against yourself. You literally *can reverse* your low opinion of yourself and start to like who you are again. Forgiveness can heal you and allow you to move on in life with great meaning and purpose. Forgiveness matters . . . and *you* will be its beneficiary.

It is time to examine the evidence. Let's move farther into this new room unlocked by the first key.

How Forgiveness Matters: What the Science Says

We will start our discussion with scientific findings, which I have been gathering since 1989. As you will see, forgiving others produces strong psychological benefits for the one who forgives.

Reduction in Psychological Depression

Suzanne Freedman and I did a scientific study in which we helped women who were incest survivors to forgive their perpetrators. As you will see below, this does not mean that we encouraged them to reconcile. They went through a 14-month forgiveness process that involved acknowledging their own anger and sadness, committing to forgive the offending person, trying to understand him as deeply as possible (which we take up with Key 4), trying as best they could to see how deeply wounded he is (not to condone or excuse him, but to better understand him), cultivating compassion when possible, and finding new meaning from what they suffered (Key 6). After the 14 months, the women, who came to us psychologically depressed, had no depression at all, similar to what happened with Kenneth. The absence of depression continued at least through the next 14 months when we reassessed their level of this challenging condition. Forgiveness made this healing possible.[1]

Despite this positive outcome, we must not jump to the conclusion that everyone who tries to forgive will be depression-free at the journey's end. Different people will have different outcomes. Yet, even for those who experience only some relief, this bit of improvement surely is better than never having tried to forgive and never experiencing any change in the level of depression.

Reduction in Anxiety

We all know how deeply uncomfortable the feeling of anxiety can be. It is hard to relax and to focus. Our bodies may get sore from muscle tension and fatigue sets in. When my colleagues and I helped people who were in a residential drug rehabilitation facility to forgive those who had treated them harshly, their anxiety not only went down, but it returned to normal levels. Their practice of forgiveness, which included the issues in Keys 3–8 here, helped return them to emotional health, which they had maintained when we reassessed them four months after the forgiveness treatment had ended.[2] We see this kind of reduction in anxiety in other

[1] Freedman, S. R., & Enright, R. D. (1996). Forgiveness as an intervention goal with incest survivors. *Journal of Consulting and Clinical Psychology*, 64(5), 983–992. http://dx.doi .org/10.1037/0022-006X.64.5.983
[2] Lin, W. F., Mack, D., Enright, R. D., Krahn, D., & Baskin, T. (2004). Effects of forgiveness

studies as well, such as the one with incest survivors described above and even with adolescents who are struggling in school.

Reduction in Unhealthy Anger

Not all anger is unhealthy. It is common to get angry when we are treated unfairly. After all, others should treat us with the respect with which we treat them. To feel anger under such circumstances is to show others that we have a sense of self-worth and expect fair treatment. However, there is also an unhealthy kind of anger that can settle into us and is not easy to reduce or eliminate. It is the kind of anger that can make us continually uncomfortable, unhappy, and even inappropriately aggressive with others. This kind of anger eventually can lead to emotional complications such as depression and to physical complications as well, including fatigue—which, in turn, can lead to a lack of exercise, weight gain, and even cardiac compromise.

Our research over the years has consistently shown that anger is reduced when people are able and willing to go through a process of forgiveness. In referring again to the study of people in the drug rehabilitation center, we saw a significant decrease in their levels of unhealthy anger after they forgave their perpetrators. In fact, they actually showed normal anger levels at the end of treatment and at our follow-up. When they were still deeply angry, before forgiveness therapy, they would engage in drinking and/or drug use to dull the pain of the cruel treatment they had endured from others and to dull the anger inside of them.

My colleagues and I also have published a study showing that forgiveness causes not only a reduction in felt anger but also improvement in the functioning of the heart, which can be affected by the level of anger a person has. We worked with men on the cardiac unit of a hospital. All of them, of course, had compromised heart functioning, and all were selected for the study because they

therapy on anger, mood, and vulnerability to substance use among inpatient substance-dependent clients. *Journal of Consulting and Clinical Psychology, 72*(6), 1114–1121. http://dx.doi.org/10.1037/0022-006X.72.6.1114; PMid:15612857 still harbored considerable anger toward at least one person who had treated them unfairly. Before forgiveness therapy, when we asked the men to tell their story of being hurt by the unjust treatment, the amount of blood flow through their hearts would decrease. After forgiveness therapy, when they retold that same story of the one who was unfair to them, the blood flow through their hearts was not negatively affected. As the head of cardiology in that hospital told us, we had helped these men to reduce the possibility of chest pains and sudden death.[3] At the time of publication, this study was the only report in the global research literature showing that practicing forgiveness leads to an improvement of a major organ in the body. The hearts were not completely restored to health by forgiveness therapy, but the therapy did play a part in aiding an already-compromised cardiac system.

As one more example of the importance of forgiveness in anger reduction, my colleagues and I have worked since 2002 with schoolteachers in the United States and Europe to provide forgiveness education in first-grade, third-grade, fifth-grade, and middle school classrooms. In research studies in Milwaukee's central city, Wisconsin, and in Belfast, Northern Ireland, the teachers deliver forgiveness education through the medium of stories, such as "Horton Hears a Who," by Dr. Seuss. In just 1 hour per week for 8–17 weeks (depending on the ages of the children), children's anger levels go from the unhealthy category to the normal level. Forgiveness helped restore these children and adolescents to emotional health.[4]

---

[3] Waltman, M. A., Russell, D. C., Coyle, C. T., Enright, R. D., Holter, A. C., & Swoboda, C. (2009). The effects of a forgiveness intervention on patients with coronary artery disease. *Psychology and Health*, 24, 11–27. http://dx.doi.org/10.1080/08870440801975127; PMid: 20186637

[4] Enright, R. D., Knutson, J. A., Holter, A. C., Baskin, T., & Knutson, C. (2007). Waging peace through forgiveness in Belfast, Northern Ireland II: Educational programs for mental health improvement of children. *Journal of Research in Education*, Fall, 63–78; Holter, A. C., Magnuson, C., Knutson, C., Knutson Enright, J. A., & Enright, R. D. (2008). The forgiving child: The impact of forgiveness education on excessive anger for elementary-aged children in Milwaukee's central city. *Journal of Research in Education*, 18, 82–93.

Decrease in Posttraumatic Stress Symptoms

Posttraumatic stress symptoms are challenging and can linger long after a difficult event has occurred in one's life. Examples of post-traumatic stress symptoms include recurring, troubling thoughts about the situation of being treated very unfairly, dreaming about what happened, and intense distress when reminded of what happened. Gayle Reed and I published a study in which she worked with women who had been emotionally abused. After the forgiveness therapy, the women's report of their post-traumatic stress symptoms went down significantly. Eight months after the therapy ended, they were still experiencing a significant reduction in the symptoms.[5]

Increased Quality of Life

The term *quality of life* refers to an overall positive sense of comfort, contentment, or happiness with one's life as it is experienced right now. Quality of life encompasses one's physical strength and health, one's psychological adjustment to life's challenges, the fulfillment of one's purpose in life, and the amount of support that one senses from important others in one's life. Forgiveness can increase benefits in all of these areas in people who take the time to work through the process. In one rather dramatic example, Mary Hansen and I helped terminally ill cancer patients to forgive those who had hurt them in the short time of four weeks. This brief time period is unusual, but in this case, the people knew that they were dying, their energy was fading, and so they did the intensive work of forgiving those in the family toward whom they were still fuming. Some of the patients had held on to this unhealthy anger for decades.

Upon forgiving those who had been very unfair to them, these

---

[5] Reed, G., & Enright, R. D. (2006). The effects of forgiveness therapy on depression, anxiety, and post-traumatic stress for women after spousal emotional abuse. *Journal of Consulting and Clinical Psychology, 74,* 920–929. http://dx.doi.org/10.1037/0022-006X.74.5.920; PMid:17032096

courageous people reported that their overall quality of life, including how they were feeling physically, was significantly improved. They even reported that their purpose in life became clearer to them because they were leaving their families more settled, more at peace because of the forgiveness that they were offering as they were dying. We saw how their actual physical condition deteriorated over those four weeks while, at the same time, their overall well-being—their reported quality of life—kept increasing. Forgiveness helped these individuals to die well.[6]

Increased Focus

When our inner world is disrupted, it is difficult to concentrate on anything other than the inner turmoil or pain. Suppose you are walking around on a sprained ankle. How is your focus on anything else as you feel the throbbing in the foot and leg? When holding on to hurt due to others' unfairness, we are emotionally and cognitively hobbled. My colleagues and I have documented a positive change in focus in a study of middle school students who were at risk for poor academic functioning because of their lack of concentration in school. In this study, led by Maria Gambaro, we asked the teachers in a middle school to identify all of the students who were about to fail in their subjects because, from the teachers' perspective, these students were so angry that they could not concentrate. We assessed their level of anger and dissatisfaction in life with psychological scales to be sure that our assessments matched the teachers' judgments.

After going through forgiveness counseling (with a process similar to the one we used with the incest survivors), these students, who were almost failing their courses, went from a typical grade of D (almost failing) to a C (meaning that they are now receiving average grades). Their forgiveness helped them to focus. And further, their focus helped them to have better relationships with oth-

---

[6] Hansen, M. J., Enright, R. D., Baskin, T. W., & Klatt, J. (2009). A palliative care intervention in forgiveness therapy for elderly terminally-ill cancer patients. *Journal of Palliative Care, 25,* 51–60. PMid:19445342

ers in the school. In this case learning to forgive aided students who were about to fall off of the academic cliff. Please note that we had what is known as a "control group" to compare with those who had forgiveness counseling. The control group received typical guidance counseling without a forgiveness component. The levels of anger in these students did not decrease, and their academic performance stayed at the D level. Forgiveness counseling, in this case, was superior to the traditional counseling methods that have been in place in schools for many decades.[7]

Increased Cooperation and Reduced Bullying

In a research project in Korea, led by Jong-Hyo Park and similar to the one just described in the United States, middle school students, some of whom were in prison at the time of the study, showed decreased aggressive behavior and bullying of others once they learned how to forgive. They also became more cooperative. Why? Each of the students had been treated with disrespect by others prior to forgiveness therapy, and they were angry. Their bullying behavior gave vent to their rage. They had been treated unfairly and now they were treating others—innocent victims—harshly, and on the pain was passed. When they were able to forgive, their unhealthy anger dissipated, and they were able to be more sensitive to others.[8] Those who bully so often have been bullied; they take their pent up anger and throw it onto others. Forgiveness stops this cycle.

Increased Self-Esteem

Too often I see a pattern in which an unfairly treated person turns his or her anger about others toward him- or herself. The result is

---

[7] Gambaro, M. E., Enright, R. D., Baskin, T. A., & Klatt, J. (2008). Can school-based forgiveness counseling improve conduct and academic achievement in academically at-risk adolescents? *Journal of Research in Education, 18,* 16–27.

[8] Park, J. H., Enright, R. D., Essex, M. J., Zahn-Waxler, C., & Klatt, J. S. (2013). Forgiveness intervention for female South Korean adolescent aggressive victims. *Journal of Applied Developmental Psychology, 20,* 393–402. http://dx.doi.org/10.1016/j.appdev.2013.06.001

low self-worth or what psychologists refer to as low self-esteem. It is part of the big lie about oneself I mentioned earlier, and it needs to be changed. Forgiveness can reverse this trend of self-criticism and even self-loathing by revealing the built-in worth of all people. As one extends forgiveness to others in the form of compassion and understanding, these come to the forgiver as well.

When the incest survivors came to us, they did not like themselves. I found their self-critical stances to be so unfair, but I now see it as all too typical. I found it unfair because, after all, each one was a victim of a horrible crime against her, and yet they had all ended up not liking who *they* are as persons. I am happy to report that after the forgiveness therapy, the women improved significantly in their self-esteem levels, and these improvements held even at the follow-up assessment 14 months later. We saw the same improvement in the study of emotionally abused women. They were able to recapture a respect for themselves, a liking of themselves following the practice of forgiveness.

Reminder 1:

Science supports the view that you can be emotionally healed from the unfair situation or situations that have been a part of your life. Forgiveness can help bring about this kind of healing for you.

Why Forgiveness Matters:
Some Observed Benefits

The following points are the general impressions I have gathered as I observe people who forgive others and thereby reclaim their lives. Forgiveness, in short, offers benefits beyond what we can "verify" through our scientific studies.

Forgiveness as a Future Protection of Your Inner World

Imagine, for a moment, the current reality in too many large cities: Alarm systems going off helter-skelter. Bars on first-floor windows. Razor wire on top of thick walls housing businesses or classrooms.

None of these attempts to protect property or persons offers protection to our inner worlds. If anything, as they protect property, they remain constant reminders to people that they are not very safe. This ever-present message can chip away at us until we are filled with anxiety and discouragement within . . . sadly without *any* sense of safety.

Forgiveness is not a naive little thing equivalent to dismantling your home's alarm system, but it does quietly allow you to take the risk to feel safe *inside* as you practice mercy (not a common word today) and experience hope and love. Forgiveness offers protection for the heart. When I use that uncommon word "mercy" throughout the book, I mean that you go beyond justice (giving what is deserved) and give the person more than what is deserved. Giving to the poor, for example, when you do not have a lot of money is an act of mercy.

Even when there is chaos reigning outside, you can experience the safe feeling within because you have a countermove to injustice, and that is to extend mercy when mercy is not coming to you. Forgiveness is somewhat like the aikido of interpersonal relations and your inner world. When your attacker comes at you, it might look like you are falling down as you practice forgiveness, but what you are really doing is using that person's momentum of aggression to throw it harmlessly over your shoulder, often much to the surprise of the one experiencing your aikido-mercy. Forgiveness protects your inner world from the attack of injustice and its effects of anger, resentment, and discouragement.

Recovery of Your Self-Worth

When we have been treated very unfairly by others over a long period of time, we sometimes can lose the vision that we have worth and deserve to be treated with respect. As we forgive, we see that all persons, even ourselves, deserve to be treated respectfully because we, like all others, have built-in worth. This knowledge then helps us to recover the truth about being respected for our very personhood. We then usually find the inner strength to recover self-worth that may have diminished slowly over time

---

Reminder 2:

Forgiveness of others is a protection for your own emotional well-being and for how you view who you are as a person.

Exercise #1: Examine Why Forgiveness Matters

Let's pause here and ask the overarching question of the chapter: Does forgiveness matter for you? What do you think so far? What is your evidence to this point to support your view? Have a little internal dialogue with yourself about this question. Please try to include information from the chapter to support your view. What is your skeptical side saying about what you have read so far? Can you counter this skepticism with good reasons why forgiveness *does* matter? Which one is winning the debate? Are you ready to consider other ideas about how forgiveness matters for all of us?

Forgiveness Restores Order

Lyllian was raising two children by herself. Her mother, addicted to drugs, stole much money from her, money she needed for the children. She fumed, and rightly so. She was working an extra job now to try to earn back some of the money. With no emotional support from others, with an angry heart, she had minimal time for her children. The house was a mess. Lyllian looked at the situation and concluded: "We pull together as a family, but this sure is chaos!" The chaos was created, in part, by a hurting, fuming heart that did not have the energy to pay attention to her children even when they were speaking to her. The injustice that she experienced from others had seized her heart and left her aching with fatigue beyond the two jobs she was working. A lack of forgiveness was contributing to disorderly behavior and to the children picking up on this and behaving in disruptive ways.

Of course, this idea is not meant to go to extremes so that we now think of forgiveness as part of a little army that magically irons shirts and polishes boots. Instead, we are talking about a quiet order first within and then expressed in behavior, a settled order that is hard to realize when beaten down by resentment and fatigue. Forgiveness can give us that added boost of energy and quietude of the mind so that we can create a more orderly world for ourselves and for those around us. Leading a life of relative order is a sign that one's heart is now more quiet and settled.

Reminder 3:

Your forgiveness can lead to more orderly thinking, feeling, and acting.

Forgiveness Prevents Disorder

Forgiveness does not only help you to clean up messes in the heart and home but also it can help prevent disorder from creeping into your life. Had Lyllian known about forgiveness and had she practiced it in the little things, she now could have brought this life-giving process into the present with her mother. The result might have been greater energy from the beginning, which would have prevented the disorder that crept into the family.

Sometimes forgiveness has a way of stopping the chaos, the disorder, before it even begins. Have you ever thought about that? Forgiveness is standing ready to help you keep an ordered life going even as others are intent on challenging you and bringing you down. Forgiveness is strong as well as gentle.

Reminder 4:

Your forgiveness can be so strong that it helps you minimize disorder.

Forgiveness Prevents Further Chaos after the Original Injustice

An admired colleague of mine lost her child to kidnapping and murder when the child was just entering her teenage years. This event was so shocking, so vicious, that it started to invade the mother's heart. She said, while smiling, that she would have gladly killed the man if she could have done so. Yet, in time she realized that her entire being was being consumed by the effects of the hatred and resentment living within her . . . and she did not like who she was becoming.

The killer was about to take a second victim—the mother—as she emotionally deteriorated under the stress and monstrous nature of the act. She wanted revenge and for a long time experienced psychological depression as she watched the rest of her family struggle with their own resentment. After many months and much effort to understand the man and offer even a glimmer of forgiveness, her downward emotional spiral began slowly to ease, and her life took on new meaning. She became a conduit of good for her other children, showing them a new way, one based on the paradox of forgiving one who was gravely unjust to her family. The children were able to see this new way and slowly to take that forgiveness into their own hearts. A life of meaning and purpose in service to others grew in the heart of the family.

The killer did not claim this family as other victims and there eventually was triumph over hatred and its dangerous psychological effects. The mother came to realize that profound injustice can kill without even touching another, but it did not happen here. There is important insight in realizing that forgiveness helps us stand against the chaos of cruelty and overcome it even when the grave injustice has had its way for a while. It no longer continues to have its way because the absence of good (the chaotic injustice) is met by patience and the struggle to forgive and it is forgiveness that seems to win in the long run.

Reminder 5:

Your forgiveness can help you stand against the worst kind of injustice so that it does not defeat you.

Exercise #2: Examine the Reminders

Let's pause now for a little while and get some exercise. Throughout this book, exercises are suggested to strengthen your inner muscles of forgiveness. Each of the exercises is designed to support and fortify a different part of forgiveness in you so that you truly can develop as a forgiver. First review each of the "Reminders":

Reminder 1: Science supports the view that you can be emotionally healed from the unfair situation or situations that have been a part of your life. Forgiveness can help bring about this kind of healing for you.

Reminder 2: Forgiveness is a protection for your own emotional well-being and for how you view who you are as a person.

Reminder 3: Your forgiveness can lead to more orderly thinking, feeling, and acting.

Reminder 4: Your forgiveness can be so strong that it helps you minimize disorder.

Reminder 5: Your forgiveness can help you stand against the worst kind of injustice so that it does not defeat you.

Now, consider this question: Which of these statements strike you as false? Perhaps you think they are unattainable for you? If you are typical of what others think, then Reminder 1 might make you feel a bit round-shouldered because you may not be feeling that the scientific results will apply to you in particular. Emotional wounds can blur any positive emotions you might otherwise experience. For now, let's just be patient with this one and not try to fight our way through to emotional improvement.

Reminder 2 might scare you, at least a little. "How can offering forgiveness to one who has hurt me," you might wonder, "actually protect *me* rather than the one who was unfair? After all, if I forgive that person, you might say that I'm accepting what he [or she] did to me. And then that person could take advantage of me—again!" As we will see shortly, to forgive another person is *not* to accept the injustice itself.

Reminders 3–5 might even discourage you a little because they deal with order and strength and struggling after goodness . . . and you probably do not have the strength yet. The strength will come in time, as you slowly begin to do the work of forgiveness.

As a brief aside, when I use the words "good" or "goodness," following Plato, I mean all that is loving, just, courageous, and wise. It sums up the growth in character. The centrality of love (*agape* in Greek) was not part of Plato's philosophy but developed over the centuries as scholars refined the original thinking of both Plato and Aristotle.

So, Then, What *Is* Forgiveness?

We are now at an important place in our forgiveness journey. If you misunderstand what forgiveness is, then you will be taking many wrong turns as we travel together. For example, suppose in considering the reminders above, you think that to forgive is to give into another's demands. This should scare you, especially if those demands are harmful or even just unreasonable. Forgiveness, in this case, would be a kind of weakness, a submission. Or, suppose you see forgiveness as "just moving on." Many see forgiveness this way, but it is not correct. You can "move on" with a great deal of resentment in your heart, which will hardly germinate hope, love, strength, and joy within you. Resentment that becomes a part of you literally can kill you, so forgiveness must be much more than "just moving on." To explore what forgiveness really is, I begin with some typical misunderstandings that people have about it, and then define it.

Forgiveness Is Not Saying "I Forgive You"

Is forgiveness basically saying, "I forgive you," and the other accepting the forgiveness? No, this is not forgiveness. You can say, "I forgive you," but deep in your heart you are carrying that resentment we just discussed, the kind that can kill you if it is deep and long-lasting. Forgiveness would not be part of goodness, if it were so superficial. Forgiveness is not only about *what* is said but also *what is in the heart.* You can genuinely forgive without ever verbalizing it, if the other person, for example, were likely to take offense.

Forgiveness Is Not Primarily about You

To this point, we have focused on your emotional healing, which I consider to be very important because it may be the primary reason why you are reading this book. As we see when examining the science, forgiveness offers the strong hope that you indeed will experience considerable emotional healing when you forgive. And yet, forgiveness, in its essence, is not something that basically is about you or done for you. Instead, forgiveness is about extending goodness toward those who have hurt you.

When each of us asks the question, "Is forgiveness basically something I do for me?", it focuses on the *consequences of forgiveness* and not on forgiveness itself. Let's separate these two—*what forgiveness is* and *what happens once we forgive*—before going any further. Because forgiveness is concerned with goodness, it is not fundamentally a self-seeking activity, as we will see shortly.

Forgiveness Does Not Deplete You Emotionally

I've been asked, "Might I get 'used up' if I continually forgive those who hurt me?" This line of thinking again suggests that to forgive is something that depletes and injures a person, rather than something centered in goodness. If "forgiveness" dries you up or depletes you in any way, then it is not something good. There are certainly false forms of forgiveness, such as trying to be seen by others as a good and forgiving person. When this is done out of pride, then an attempt to see the humanity in the one who acted unjustly may be missing in the "forgiver." In this scenario, a lot of resentment remains in the heart—and it is the resentment that depletes you.

Forgiveness Is Not Finding Excuses for the Offending Person's Behavior

"Isn't forgiveness just about finding a good excuse for why the other person acted that way?", you might wonder. The short answer is no. Forgiveness is not about putting one's head in the sand and playing pretend. Forgiveness stands in the truth that what happened was unfair, it is still unfair, and it will always be unfair. At the same time, the one who forgives willfully tries to abandon resentment and to think of the other person as fully human in spite of what he or she did.

Forgiveness Is Offered to Persons, Not to Inanimate Objects

As you can see in the point above, we only forgive persons because in the forgiving we attempt to think of those forgiven as fully human. Further, to forgive is to try to abandon resentment. We have resentment when someone acts unjustly toward us. We thus do not forgive inanimate objects such as hurricanes, for example, because they cannot act unjustly nor can we try to see them as "fully human."

Forgiveness Is Not a Quick Formula You Can Follow

"Can't you just tell me how to forgive, and I do it, then it is over?" I have heard this kind of plea many times over the years. It is as if we are seeking the "forgiveness pill," something that quickly does the work for us. Yet, to forgive is to engage in struggle toward greater understanding of the one who was unjust and so there are no quick fixes for most of us. Yes, some people can experience spontaneous forgiveness, but that is so very rare. For most of us, we travel a path before we end up forgiving. That is why we have the eight keys of forgiveness with us. We have to use the eight keys to enter the various rooms and walk the path before we can say, "I truly have forgiven this person."

What Is Forgiveness?

I keep saying that forgiveness is connected to goodness. The kind of goodness that is central to forgiveness is love. As we forgive in its deepest sense, we try as best we can to love the one who has hurt us. This is an extremely tall order, and I do not expect you to hit this target right now. It can take a very long time to cultivate love in your heart for those who have hurt you. When I use the word *love* here, I mean that you want what is best for the other person. There is a sense of service here, in that you are willing to take steps for his or her betterment in this life. Again, achieving this attitude, this stance, takes time, effort, practice, and strength. We are all imperfect people, and so love may take a form that is less than perfect, such as cultivating respect for the person, not because of what he or she did, but in spite of this. The love might take the form of kindness or generosity rather than full-blown service for the benefit of those who have hurt you.

A specific manifestation of this kind of love in the process of forgiveness is mercy. *Mercy* is offering to others what they have not deserved because of their lack of respect, kindness, generosity, and love toward you. Even though they did not extend these to you, it is the case in forgiveness that you do give these to those who have hurt you. That is mercy: to give what was *not* given to you.

So on the path of goodness along the journey of forgiveness we start with the largest form of goodness: love. We then exercise a particular form of love: mercy. We then extend that love and mercy specifically to those who have been unfair to us. This is forgiveness.

For example, consider Nathaniel's situation in which he was physically abused by his brother, Philip, when they both were in high school. Philip's hot temper and explosive outbursts of aggression made it almost impossible for Nathaniel to have a healthy relationship with his brother, even when they were adults. Nonetheless, Nathaniel struggled to forgive his brother from the heart, which was not easy, requiring months of effort with the aid of a counselor. As part of those counseling sessions, he tried to see Philip as a person of worth. As he forgave, Nathaniel continued to realize that his brother's behavior was wrong and will always be considered wrong, but those actions were not to be the foundation from which Nathaniel exclusively thought about his brother. His brother was and is more than his aggressive actions. This kind of thinking prepared Nathaniel for reconciliation with Philip, if he was willing to change.

Nathaniel waited for several years in the hope of a reconciliation which came suddenly when Philip was diagnosed with terminal cancer. Because Nathaniel had done the prior work of forgiveness, this helped him to go to the hospital and become involved in his brother's care. He spent time daily assisting with feeding Philip and giving him support. These were acts of mercy, of service love, which at first were difficult because of the harsh treatment to which Nathaniel was subjected for years. His generosity to Philip helped them both during this time of transition. They rediscovered the mutual affection of brotherly love for one another, which is easier to give than service love. When Philip passed away, Nathaniel reported that he was happy that he forgave because now he was only mourning. Had he not forgiven, the mourning would have been mixed with deep resentment, a combination that he knew would have been very challenging for him.

As you can see, when you forgive, you see clearly that the other was unfair and did hurt you. So you are not condoning or excusing what he or she did. You are not forgetting what happened to you. Yet you are not remembering with a clenched fist and a tightened jaw. You are remembering with love and mercy.

All of this, the love and mercy and forgiveness, starts within you, in your heart. These qualities flow from you to the other, again as best you can as an imperfect person. When you forgive, you may or may not reconcile. To forgive and to reconcile cannot be the same thing because reconciliation is a kind of negotiation strategy in which two or more people make their way back together again in mutual trust. It is centered in behavior. Forgiveness, in contrast, is first and foremost centered in the heart and then, once it matures there, flows outward to others. A major goal of forgiveness is to reconcile, but the other person might reject that offer even when we are extending love and mercy.

When we forgive, we willingly and deliberately offer goodness to those who have been unfair to us. The goodness comes in the form of love and mercy even when the others have not been fair, loving, or merciful to us. This offer is a free choice on the part of the one who forgives.

Reminder 6:

When you forgive, you have mercy on those who have been unjust to you. You may or may not reconcile with the one who acted unjustly.

It is time now to consider some questions that are typically asked when people enter this forgiveness room with the first key.

Frequently Asked Questions

Question 1

"It seems that forgiveness is a passive activity because everything takes place in the heart. Is this the case?"

No, actually, it is not the case. Forgiveness only begins in the heart and does not stay there. It flows from the heart to others, we must remember. Others are the recipients of your love, mercy, and forgiveness.

Question 2

"Am I, as the forgiver, left out of all of this? It seems like I am doing all of the giving and the other is doing all of the getting and it does not seem fair."

We have to recall the paradox of forgiveness: As we forgive, the science shows that we, as forgivers, benefit a great deal in terms of renewed emotional health. The giving of love and mercy does not deplete us; it renews us.

Question 3

"But where is all of this protection you are talking about? I'm feeling very vulnerable when I think of having mercy on someone whom I cannot trust."

A major mistake by many is what I call "either–or" thinking. When you forgive, you do not put justice aside. Forgiveness and justice grow together. As you forgive, ask something of the other person. Ask for fairness. As you forgive, your quest for fairness may be better served than if you asked with those clenched fists and the tightened jaw.

Question 4

"How long will this take?"

It depends on how often you have practiced forgiveness in the past. The more practice, the quicker the new journey will be, but again please realize that we are all imperfect and so struggle is always likely. The deeper the hurt, the more time it will take. If the one who hurt you is obligated to love you, such as a parent or a marriage partner, then the betrayal is greater than if a stranger hurts you. Betrayals take longer than ordinary slights and injustices by others who also are imperfect but try hard to get it right.

Other questions are likely to come up for you. You can ask the questions directly to me at the International Forgiveness Institute, Inc. (*website*: internationalforgiveness.com). We have a section entitled, "Ask Dr. Forgiveness." Please feel free to use this option for your questions. I will try to respond quickly to you.

Some Forgiveness Heroes

Let's take a little time to meet some real-life forgiveness heroes—those who have fought the battles of injustice through the love and mercy that are forgiveness. Try to see their vibrancy, their hope, their enthusiasm for life. For each of them, forgiveness matters and in some cases saved their lives . . . and the lives of others. Let yourself feel inspired by these heroes so that you can think about your own ability to forgive and press on with your own forgiveness journey.

Marietta Jaeger

In this chapter you already met a woman who forgave the murderer of her daughter. That heroic person is Marietta Jaeger. You can view her testimony to the power of forgiveness in a documentary film, *From Fury to Forgiveness*, first shown on the Discovery

Channel in 1994. You will see at first a distraught and emotionally beaten-down Marietta in home-movie film footage at the
time of the tragedy. She saw her family melting down right before
her eyes because the search for Susie was taking so long. During
the year following Susie's death, Marietta worked on forgiveness
to such a degree that the marvelously unexpected happened. On
the exact one-year anniversary of Susie's passing, the man who
killed her telephoned Marietta to taunt her. Yet, her heart, already
filled with forgiveness, led to her asking: "What can I do for
you?" Imagine such a question in this context of murder and now
taunting.

The man was so taken aback that he stayed on the phone long
enough for detectives to trace the origin of his call and to capture
him. Forgiveness led to the capture of someone who, upon further questioning, admitted to multiple murders. Marietta's forgiveness likely put a stop to his future killings. Now working
against the death penalty, Marietta's vitality for her life's purpose
gives deep meaning to that life, which she passes on to others in
the form of this message: We are all special, unique, and irreplaceable, including those who murder. Of course, it took her a
long time to arrive at this point in her journey, but as you can see,
it was fully and indefatigably accomplished.

Forgiveness in this case mattered because it saved a mother's
life and probably saved the lives of future victims. Marietta's forgiveness likely saved some lives on death row as well, as Marietta
continues to work tirelessly against the death penalty.

Martin Luther King, Jr.

In his book, *Strength to Love*, the civil rights hero talked repeatedly
of loving one's enemies. We have to realize the context in which
these statements were made. As he was writing this book, his home
was being firebombed, threatening his spouse and children. Yet, he
stood against the injustice of racial hatred and its insidious manifestation in segregation—and he let love be stronger than resentment.

You can see Dr. King's view of forgiveness in the title of his first chapter, "A Tough Mind and a Tender Heart." This is where we are heading with our keys to forgiveness. You develop a tough mind by saying, "What happened to me should not have happened!" and yet your heart responds with love, mercy, and forgiveness. When you deliberately offer goodness in the face of your own pain, you are showing great strength and courage, not weakness.

According to Dr. King, the hard-hearted person never accomplishes the love and compassion needed to truly forgive. He or she never actually sees people as people, but instead as means to an end, something to be manipulated. Dr. King saw clearly that all, even the unjust, are persons and therefore must be treated as such. He saw this while he and his family were under great duress. This takes such inner strength.

In that first chapter of his book, Dr. King warned his followers that they must respond to the civil rights movement with the combination of a tough mind and a tender heart because that combination can produce social change, and it can do so on a smaller scale, such as in your own family.

In yet another of his books, *A Knock at Midnight,* Dr. King makes the point that whenever people gather, there will be many there with broken hearts. If you are one of those, do not run from the fact that you have a broken heart, he says. Acknowledge it, at least to yourself and bear the reality of that brokenness. In other words, stand up to the fact that your heart is broken. Dr. King's heart was broken, too. His people were taunted and denigrated on a grand scale, yet his heart was big enough to die so that others' hearts in the future would not be so broken. It was one of his goals that people walk in forgiveness, and he gave his life for that conviction.

Forgiveness in this case mattered to an entire race of American people who have been asking for civil rights. Can you imagine how the civil rights movement might have gone if Dr. King had not possessed such a forgiving heart?

Corrie ten Boom

Cornelia "Corrie" ten Boom, along with other family members in her Dutch community, helped Jewish people to escape the evil of the Holocaust during World War II. She was arrested and sent to a concentration camp in the Netherlands and then eventually to the hellish women's concentration camp in Ravensbruck, Germany. Both her brother and sister passed away while imprisoned by the Nazis. Her book, *The Hiding Place,* refers to the house, and the secret room within that house, in which the family sheltered Jewish people from the Nazis and which subsequently led to her arrest and harsh imprisonment.

When she was released in 1945 one of her purposes was to give talks about love and forgiveness. As she relates in the final pages of her book, one of her greatest life challenges occurred after she had just completed such a talk in Munich. She had no idea that the SS officer who had abused her years before in the Ravensbruck concentration camp was in the audience that night. He greeted her outside with a hand extended to her. He asked for forgiveness. Now it was time for her to show that she practiced the forgiveness that she preached. Yet, she had no forgiveness within her to give.

After saying a short prayer, she, by her own report, felt a kind of electrical current pass from her shoulder, down her arm, and into her hand, which she extended in forgiveness to the SS officer. She felt a love in her heart for this man and the love almost overwhelmed her. She offered him forgiveness.

Cornelia's report is unusual in that her forgiveness was instantaneous and therefore rare. For most of us imperfect people, forgiveness is a struggle of submission to the mercy that we hope to give. It takes time and effort. I relate her story to you as a form of encouragement. Forgiveness sometimes surprises us in very positive ways.

Forgiveness mattered to the SS officer and to Corrie herself who was released from bottled-up anger. Forgiveness in this case has mattered to millions of people who have read the book and seen a film based on the events described in the book. She reached a multitude with a story of hope, love, and joy in the face of the most gruesome of circumstances. Forgiveness matters here because it can inspire the rest of us to press onward toward the goal of offering mercy to those who have not exercised justice toward us.

Joseph

The chronicler of early Hebrew history simply refers to this biblical figure as Joseph, the son of Jacob. Joseph's story has captivated people for thousands of years, up to the present day when a broadway play, *The Coat of Many Colors*, was written to tell his story. Whether seen as allegory or as part of history, the story carries much weight in showing the importance of forgiveness for an entire community.

The youngest of 12 siblings, his 10 half-brothers and 1 full brother, Benjamin, were jealous of the attention lavished on him by their father. Their resentment overwhelmed them to such a degree that they seized Joseph and threw him down a well in an attempt to murder him. Quickly changing their minds, they pulled him out of the well and then sold him into slavery in Egypt.

A series of startling events in Egypt eventually led to Joseph's position of authority in the government. As that point in time, the Hebrew nation was experiencing famine and the 10 half-brothers traveled to Egypt seeking mercy from the government in the form of supplies to avert disaster within their community. The magistrate whom they consulted was Joseph himself, who recognized them, but they did not recognize him because, of course, they thought he was a slave somewhere far from governmental power.

Joseph, unlike Corrie ten Boom, did not experience anything even close to spontaneous and immediate forgiveness. He instead threw the 10 relatives into prison. When he heard them lamenting their fate, blaming it on how they treated their brother Joseph so many years ago, he wept. Because he wanted to see his full brother, Benjamin, he ordered all but one of the half-brothers to bring Benjamin to Egypt. The other he kept in the Egyptian prison to assure their return.

When they did return and he saw Benjamin, Joseph wept a second time. Although his heart was softening, he played a trick on Benjamin. After giving them supplies sufficient to protect the Hebrew nation, he hid a silver goblet in Benjamin's saddlebag. When they had traveled a good distance, Joseph and soldiers of the Egyptian army rode up to them, looked into Benjamin's saddlebag, and accused him of stealing. At this point, one of the half-brothers tore his own clothing and asked Joseph to take him instead of Benjamin.

This act of courage and mercy on the half-brother's part so affected Joseph that he wept once again. Upon this third weeping (the number three is a symbol of perfection), he revealed himself as Joseph, embraced those who wanted to murder him years ago, and gave them sufficient supplies to save the Hebrew nation.

Forgiveness in this case mattered greatly to this large family that now was reunited in the heart. At the same time, Joseph's forgiveness literally helped to save an entire ethnic group. The Hebrew nation and subsequent monotheistic groups that have origins in the Hebrew writings owe a great debt of gratitude to Joseph. His forgiveness played a part in preserving and passing on the monotheistic (one God) tradition for billions of people.

Forgiveness matters and sometimes in ways we will never see because the love flows through generation after generation, as it did for Joseph, his brothers, the Hebrew nation, and beyond. Let us end this chapter with more questions that typically follow stories such as these.

More Questions

Question 5

"Forgiveness as you describe it here seems like an ideal that few can master. What about me, who may not be a 'forgive-

ness hero'? And do you have to be a religious person to forgive?"

Forgiveness is for the imperfect and so we all practice it imper-
fectly. If we only looked, for example, at the best basketball players
in the world and said, "I will never play that well," few of us would
ever play the game even for occasional enjoyment. It is the same
with forgiveness. We do not throw up our hands in despair because
Martin Luther King, Jr., gave his life in his struggle to bring about
great change through a nonviolent stand of patience, love, and
mercy. We do not turn away because Joseph turned with love
toward his murderous brothers.

Try to accept as best you can wherever you are today in the
forgiveness process. As with our basketball example, the more you
practice, the better you will get . . . and you need not be perfect to
benefit emotionally from the practice.

Regarding the question of religion, we have to realize that
forgiveness is centered in goodness, as I had mentioned earlier
in the chapter. There are many ways to be good, such as acting
fairly (which is the practice of the moral virtue of justice), giving
to the poor (the moral virtue of altruism), and even putting up
with minor annoyances from loved ones (tolerance). Most of us
try to be fair and, at least at times, altruistic and tolerant. Why
should it be different with forgiveness as you try to practice
mercy toward those who have not been fair to you? You are practicing a particular moral virtue from a position of your own pain.
Every person on the planet experiences this kind of pain and has
the capacity to understand forgiveness and to practice it if he or
she wishes. Yes, people from different religions and cultures
might practice forgiveness differently with different rituals, but
down deep it is the essence of forgiveness that they are all practicing.

In our scientific work, my colleagues and I have helped the
religiously indifferent, the agnostic, the atheist, as well as the religious person to understand and to practice forgiveness. We all

hurt; we all need forgiveness; and we are all capable of practicing this moral virtue.

Question 6

"Is it possible that I might forgive, then change my mind, then forgive again? This seems to have happened to Joseph in that he was hard on the brothers, then wept, but repeated the pattern of harshness."

This question is basically asking if there is one straight path to the end point of forgiveness for everyone who walks this path. The short answer is no. When you walk the forgiveness path, you definitely do certain things that everyone on this path will do, such as practicing mercy toward the other. Yet we do so differently. For some, it is hard to start the journey because of the intense anger. For others, the path is smooth until the other once again is unfair and then, presto, the anger is back with a fury! For others still, like Corrie ten Boom, it seems that there hardly is a journey at all because the trip was so quick. Yet even she was traveling the path of forgiveness with each talk she gave about it. We all travel this road a little differently, and you yourself will find out that each trip you take down this road is a bit different from the previous one. Be open to surprises on the journey.

Question 7

"In the case of Marietta Jaeger, Corrie ten Boom, and Joseph, the cruelty they experienced eventually ceased. But what if in my case the person I have in mind is continually hurting me? What then?"

You have a greater forgiveness challenge when the other insists on being continually unfair. I have two suggestions for you. First, forgiveness is all the more necessary under these circumstances because the resentments can build to very high levels if you are not careful. The 20th injustice from a particular person can be more damaging than the 1st because of this accumulated resentment. Continual forgiveness, though a tough task, can help you to stay emotionally healthy. Second, please remember to take the moral virtue of justice along with you. Forgive the person, yes, but then ask something of him or her. Ask for fairness and if you are practicing forgiveness, then what you ask is likely to be reasonable rather than a pound of flesh from him or her. As a last resort, please remember that when you forgive, it is not necessary to reconcile if the other is a danger to you. It may be necessary to remove yourself from any physical proximity from this person to preclude further hurt. Forgiveness does not mean you are a punching bag.

BECOME FORGIVINGLY FIT

Power over others is ultimately an impostor. At first, it can overwhelm and dominate so that it seems to have taken hold permanently. Yet love always seems to overcome it. Is your vision driven by power or by love?

This second key is intended to positively change your inner world before you start the forgiveness process. In the beginning, we are not quite ready to start the forgiveness process. First comes the preparation of examining who hurt you, what comprises your inner world of pain, and how you have reacted to that pain. I do not want to unlock that door yet as a protection for you. We can face pain, head on, some of the time. At other times it is better to be prepared and then face the pain. This is one of those be-prepared-first rooms: a forgiveness gym, so to speak. There is the treadmill, the stair-stepper, and the stationary bike. Oh, and there is the rowing machine.

Yes, I know, I pointed out all of the cardio equipment first. This is because we have to be sure that your heart . . . your psychological heart . . . is in great shape for the rest of the journey. We need you to be forgivingly fit first and the best way to do that is to exercise mind and heart, body and soul—and then face the pain of others withdrawing love from you and having no mercy on you.

Consider two athletic analogies to help you see the importance of this inner transformation before beginning your journey of forgiveness. The late Herb Brooks is famous for leading the U.S. men's hockey team to a gold medal in the 1980 Winter

Olympics as they defeated the USSR team in the semifinals. "The legs feed the wolves, gentlemen," he would repeatedly say in practices, meaning that you have to be strongly fit if you are to defeat the machine that is the USSR hockey team. He focused on fitness first and then the skills of hockey—and it worked. This chapter is meant to help prepare you in a similar way. Your being fit in a psychological sense for this task will help you triumph.

Another athletic legend is Norman Dale, who led the small Milan High School boys' basketball team to the Indiana State Championship in 1954. The film *Hoosiers*, starring Gene Hackman, is loosely based on his story. A key to Dale's success was his emphasis on physical fitness. In practice, the team wanted to have fun and play the game. Dale emphasized fitness first, fundamentals second, and then playing the game once these were in place. As with Herb Brooks, it worked. The legs feed the wolves.

In your case, I am talking about the fitness of your heart because the heart is at the center of human determination, will, and emotion. It is where you summon your strength to face life's challenges no matter what. You will find it difficult to do this until you are fit, so that is the goal of this chapter: to strengthen your heart and let it grow a few sizes in its love and generosity. We will then use the third key to take this fitness into our next room, a hard room to be in because you will confront your pain. So, with all of this in mind, let's start with a couple of case studies that center on heart health in its emotional sense.

Case Study: The Loss of a Son

Marsha and Juan were the dedicated parents of three children: Eduardo, age 17; Susanna, age 13; and Anna, age 10. When the police officer came to their door on that fateful winter night, Marsha's heart sank. *One of the children is in trouble,* she thought. She quickly wiped her hands on the dishtowel and answered the door. "May we come in?" one of the officers asked in a too-sober way for her liking. Trembling now, Marsha let them into the living room.

The officers proceeded to explain that their oldest child, Eduardo, had died from using cocaine. He was at a party in which three other youths had pressured him to "show his courage" and try it for the first time in his life. It was more than Eduardo's body could take, and he had passed away by the time the paramedics arrived.

The three youths were taken into custody. Nothing, of course, that would now happen to them would be sufficient to bring back Eduardo, Marsha thought bleakly. She knew the boys responsible, and she was shocked that they were users of this dangerous drug.

Both Marsha and Juan were numbed by the news. *How could this happen? We were not there to comfort our son. What will we tell the children and the grandparents? How do we live without our son?*

Marsha and Juan were overcome with grief and rage. Their firstborn son, with his entire life ahead of him, was now gone. There was nothing left but his music player, some headphones, a baseball bat, and some books in his room. The silence especially overwhelmed them. There was no voice to come back to them as they thought about Eduardo or, even in their grief, called his name. Silence . . . and it was not going to end.

Juan's rage was intense. No sleep, little eating, no exercise, and no will to serve the family. He did not know how to forgive because his own parents passed to him a legacy of a strong temper. He frequently let loose with that now.

After more than two years, when Marsha asked him to forgive the three youths and even Eduardo himself for his poor choice that night, Juan only became angrier. He saw her request as an effort to squelch his need for justice and to do something for his son and for future victims who could succumb to the peer pressure. Yet, he did not have the strength to move forward, outside of this room of rage that he had created for himself. And in that imprisoned room he stayed—until he died, early, of stress-related causes.

One drug and three adolescents who exerted intense peer

pressure played a part in killing two people that night: Eduardo and his father. No one else drew the connection between Juan's early death by heart failure and the fateful night 12 years earlier. Marsha was the only one to see it. She was well aware that Juan's enduring despondency had led to his overeating, to his sleep disturbances, and to his lack of exercise. She knew what and who had killed him.

Juan was not prepared for what happened. The love withdrawn from him made him withdraw love all the more toward others and toward himself. He became a prisoner of his own choosing because he refused, at every turn, Marsha's pleas to forgive. So Marsha now had to deal with the loss of her son and the early death of her husband, one by the violent act of a drug, the other by the unseen action in Juan's own heart. He was eaten away from the inside . . . and it could have been avoided. Juan was not forgivingly fit when the tragedy happened, and he could not find his way to the emotional cardiac unit of forgiveness. Marsha was convinced that had he done the forgiveness work, his life would have been 100% different. She concluded the same for the family, which now had to continue the journey of life without a husband and father.

In Juan's case, the injustice against him proved to be stronger than his love. The injustice defeated him.

Case Study: The Amish and Nickel Mines, Pennsylvania

Charles Roberts was a husband and father of three children when he entered the Amish one-room schoolhouse, West Nickel Mines School, in Lancaster, Pennsylvania, on October 2, 2006. He shot 10 girls, killing 5 of them, and then himself. His wife, Maria, talking about the tragedy for the first time to ABC News on September 30, 2013, revealed that he was deeply depressed at the loss of their first daughter and blamed God for this. His murderous actions, she said, were his mentally ill way of getting back at God.

This tragedy is unspeakable in its gravity. All of a sudden and without warning, the Amish community, and especially the families directly affected by the murders, were confronted with evil. What startled the world was the way in which the entire Amish community responded. As a group, about 30 Amish community members attended Charles's funeral, comforted his widow, and even set up a charitable fund for his children. The lavish outpouring of compassion was stunning to a global world unused to such astounding open-heartedness.

I recall getting numerous phone calls from the media in the coming weeks following this evil event. The gist of many of these calls was this:

"The Amish are faking it, right?"
"No one can forgive that quickly under these circumstances!"
"Once the cameras stop rolling, the Amish community will be seething with anger, right?"

I was somewhat taken aback by the skepticism pouring from the media. So many of those who interviewed me refused to believe what they were seeing. Their reactions challenged me and so I began to look more carefully into the Amish culture. This is what I found. The Amish faith encourages daily family prayer and some of these prayers revolve around forgiving others. When the tragedy happened, individuals, families, and the community were already forgivingly fit, but few outside that community were looking closely enough to recognize this. And that is precisely why the interviewers were so skeptical. They did not have on their radar the possibility that an entire community would practice forgiveness on a daily basis. This community *did* practice forgiveness daily—and it worked far beyond most people's capacity to even imagine.

The outpouring of kindness captivated people around the world. The story is now told in the award-winning film, *The Power of Forgiveness*, and in numerous other films and books describing the tragedy and the culture that absorbed so much pain.

These kinds of stories show that forgiveness has a way of positively influencing others who observe those in the act of forgiving.

In this case, Charles Roberts's mother, Terri, had to work on forgiving her own son. She was drawn to the love in the Amish community and now volunteers to help one of the victims who sustained profound injuries and needs basic care in grooming and nutrition. In this way Terri gives love back to those who showed love to her and her family. The forgivingly fit hearts of the Amish proved to be a protection for their own community and beyond.

There is a stark contrast between how Charles Roberts reacted to the challenging life event of losing his daughter and how the Amish community reacted to losing five daughters with five more maimed. Being forgivingly fit or not when tragedy strikes matters greatly.

Seven Principles for Becoming Forgivingly Fit

Seven qualities, if they are alive within you, will help you to become more forgivingly fit. These qualities are so important that, as you practice them, you will be strengthening and increasing your ability to forgive, and perhaps even transforming your character as a person. I discuss each of these fully and provide exercises with which you can train your forgiveness muscles:

- Make a commitment to do no harm.
- Cultivate a clearer vision.
- Understand and practice love.
- Understand and practice mercy.
- Practice forgiveness itself in small ways each day.
- Practice being consistent in your forgiveness.
- Persevere in your practice of forgiveness each day.

Principle 1: Make a Commitment to Do No Harm

You may be wondering what it is you are committing to. The first issue is this: Commit to doing no harm to those who have harmed you. This is not to ask you to stop talking about the person with others. Instead it is to ask you to refrain from talking disparagingly about the person to others. As you may see, I am not asking you to have an outpouring of goodness right now toward that person. Instead, I am asking you to *refrain from the negative*. This is actually a big step in forgiving, because you are turning away from the eye-for-an-eye stance that is at the root of so much conflict in the world. Instead you are making possible the development of goodness within you for the one who hurt you. The next part of this commitment comes in the form of the first exercise in this chapter.

Exercise #1: Build Your Forgiveness Muscles: Committing to Forgiveness

In one of our research studies we posed this question to adults who had already forgiven someone for a serious offense: "What was the most difficult part of the entire forgiveness journey for you?" The most frequent answer was this: "making that commitment to forgive the one who hurt me."

If you think about it, this response makes sense because the process is so new, the nerves are raw, and so the reaching out to an offending person is really, *really* hard. Now to our exercise. All you have to do in this exercise is answer *yes* or *no* to the following questions, which are based on our definition of forgiveness in Key 1. You don't have to *do* anything else.

- Are you willing to extend goodness of some kind to the one who hurt you? (This might include eye contact or a smile or a kind gesture of some kind. I am not asking you to actually do any of this at this point. I am only asking if you are *willing* to do this at some time in the future.)
- Are you willing to see that an end point to forgiving is to love even a little? (Again, I am only asking for your

understanding here, not an actual demonstration of love toward the person.)

- Are you willing to understand more deeply what love is and to practice it in the hope of giving some of this at some time in the future to the one who harmed you?
- Are you willing to explore more deeply what mercy is?
- Are you willing, once you understand it better, to perhaps practice mercy toward the person? Again, mercy is going beyond justice (giving what is deserved) to give more than what is deserved. To try to be kind to those who are unkind to you is an example of mercy.
- Are you willing to extend goodness toward this person, knowing that he or she was not good to you?
- Are you aware that forgiveness is a free choice on your part?
- Are you willing to freely choose to forgive without letting others' pressure lead you falsely into it?
- Are you willing to try all of this through your own pain?

Reminder 7:

Many people find that making the commitment to forgive is the hardest part of the journey.

Principle 2: Cultivate a Clearer Vision

Let's start with a very large question: What is your basic view of humanity? Who are all these people walking around planet Earth with you? How can we define this large body we call humanity? I am asking, in essence, *what is a person?*

When I use the words *clearer vision,* I am challenging you to see that each person on this planet is special, unique, and irreplaceable. We can come to this conclusion either through faith or through the rationalism of atheism/agnosticism.

In a faith-based view people typically have this vision: All people are made in the image and likeness of God. In an atheist/agnostic perspective, people have this vision: By the process of evolution, humanity has evolved in such a way that each person has unique DNA that is passed to the next generation. Once a particular person dies, this uniqueness ceases.

Most of us are so busy that we rarely ponder such large questions. We have jobs and families to manage, stressors to endure, goals to accomplish. Yet taking time to consider this one large question is essential to your forgiveness journey. It is not a matter of idle philosophical musing. Developing this kind of clearer vision takes time that is well worth spent.

Reminder 8:

Each person is special, unique, and irreplaceable. It takes time and effort to understand this fundamental point.

Principle 3: Understand and Practice Love

When I use the word *love*, I am not talking about romantic love of any kind. Instead, I am talking about the kind of love that Mother Teresa showed to the poor people of Calcutta as she went into the streets to rescue and care for the sick and dying. She was giving of herself in service to others. When Gandhi went on hunger strikes for his people in India, he was showing this kind of love that is *in service* to others. The mother who is up all night with a sick child, the adult child who takes care of an elderly parent, the wealthy person who gives lavishly to a children's hospital are all showing the kind of service love that I mean here.

This kind of love is harder to master than, say, the feeling of mutual admiration seen in an engaged couple. It is harder because it costs the one who loves and sometimes there is no reciprocation of that love. Yet the person exercising this service love presses forward nonetheless. As with the idea of clearer vision, this kind of love takes practice and patience to be brought to maturity.

Reminder 9:

Service love is the kind of love in which the person gives of the self to others. It takes time and practice to get to such a point in one's life.

Exercise #2: Practicing Small Acts of Love

For today, be aware of at least three opportunities that you have to put a little more service love into the world. For example, you might take the time to smile at a cashier who seems tired and stressed on the job. Even though tired, you might take a little extra time with a child who needs your attention. You might want to gather the family and together choose a worthwhile charity and donate money. What else might you consider today as practice in love?

Principle 4: Understand and Practice Mercy

Mercy is one variant of what I am calling *service love*. Mercy occurs when you are in a position of influence or even power but you then do not exercise that power over the other. There are two patterns of showing mercy. The first is "merciful restraint," in which you refrain from doing something that is seen as negative by the other person. Here is an example: A parent sends a misbehaving child to his or her room for an hour as a well-deserved correction of the child's inappropriate behavior, but then reduces this to a half hour. The parent is having mercy on the child. The parent refrains from the negative (of more time in the room).

The second form of mercy involves the giving of something positive to the one who hurt you. Here is an example: A coworker talks about you behind your back, embarrassing you by making a false accusation. After correcting the person (which is justice and not mercy), you warmly extend your hand in an act of friendship and respect.

When you develop clearer vision, service love, merciful restraint, and mercy itself toward someone who has inflicted pain on you, then you are forgiving. Of all the moral virtues in the world (such as justice, patience, kindness, and generosity, as examples), forgiveness is the hardest because you give to those who hurt you and that is never easy. Exercises to strengthen these attributes in you will be coming later in the book.

Reminder 10:

Mercy is a variant of service love that is extended to the person who has caused you pain and takes patience and effort to master.

Intermission: Pride and Power

I would like for us to pause here to consider the two major obstacles to becoming forgivingly fit: pride and lust for power. Over the years, I have found that these two tendencies create the strongest challenges to growth in forgiveness, to advancing as a forgiver. Get to know these two so well that you can spot them in yourself and in others whenever they occur.

Let's examine each and then engage in some exercises to strengthen you against these foes to your growth in forgiveness.

Pride

C. S. Lewis, the author of *The Chronicles of Narnia*, once commented that pride is a sense of wanting to move people around like little chess pieces. He further said that pride is one of the most annoying characteristics that we see in other people—but rarely see it in ourselves. Pride puts the self first in one's heart. When the self is placed first but comes in last, envy (wanting what someone else has), jealousy (fear that you are not liked, such as being jealous of a friend whom your romantic partner might like), and anger can erupt in that heart and spill over to others, hurting them. You may have been hurt by people who were operating from a position of pride. And if pride is too strong in you, it will be hard for you to let go of your resentments.

Power

If pride is wanting to move others around like little chess pieces, then power, when it is distorted in meaning and misused, is the actual manipulation of people to suit the mover's needs; it is the taking advantage of others for one's own gain. Is it an exaggeration to say that the modern heart is bathed in pride and power to such an extent that too many people no longer see how much of these they carry into the world each day? What is the endpoint for modern societies? Toward what goals do adults in modern societies strive? What kinds of achievement equal success? For example, if we contrasted a social worker who helps single parents feed and clothe their children with a multi-millionaire who is on television frequently, which would contemporary people choose as the most admired and successful? Money is likely to trump service that is done basically behind the scenes. One of these individuals may be acting to seize power. The other is acting out of service love. Of course, neither may be misusing power, but which one is more likely to do so or at least be tempted to do so?

Here is another contrast. Who is more admired: a professional athlete who wins championships (dominates the opposition, in other words) or a middle-aged person who walks with a limp, is not athletic, but gives anonymously to the poor on a consistent basis? Power tends to win our admiration without our even giving it much thought because its pursuit is embedded in the norms of modern culture. And even if the athlete gives lavishly to hospitals or schools behind the scenes, it is his or her power that we admire and that the media cover, less frequently bothering with the behind-the-scenes acts of love.

Deliberate seeking of power over others is at odds with the

clearer vision we discussed above. Control, influence, domination, looking for an edge and a way to win simply do not align with the expansive view of personhood that comes with clearer vision. We will have blurred vision if we constantly see others in terms of how we can win or extract or gain something from them. There is no thought to the equality of persons in any true sense here. By *equality* I do not mean that we all have the same talents or should get the same wage, no matter the job. Instead, I mean that every person on the planet is special, unique, and irreplaceable. A person in a position of power over others would not agree. If someone were in the way of a goal pursued by a power-seeking person, he or she somehow would be removed, regardless of the consequences to that disposable person.

You may be steeped in power norms in your corner of society. Many of us are. These norms are at odds with service love, however, because with service love, you give of yourself rather than take. The stance of service love may be seen as weakness, as religious fanaticism, or even as a kind of self-destructive behavior by some, when in truth it is simply a good way to live. Those who operate from a position of power do not understand service love. They do not have the eyes to see with clearer vision.

But, you might ask, isn't there benign power or what we might call good power? Influence and authority are very different from the kind of power over others that we are discussing here. A teacher has influence over the students because of superior knowledge, but a teacher never should act in such a way as to use the students for his or her own ends. C. S. Lewis struggled for most of his adult life with one schoolmaster who was a tyrant, scarring many of his students for their entire lives. This was not authority, but the exercise of raw power.

Parents have authority over their children, otherwise the children literally could die from bad choices, but parents never should act in such a way as to use the children for their own ends. Power over others does that.

I have known people who are convinced that the end point of human existence is the pursuit of power, even when they themselves do not like what they see. "It's just the way it is" is a statement I have heard all too often. I have even heard it from an inner-city gang member who did not like what he saw as a "fact of life," but he felt that he had to live his life according to what he saw as the "law of power" to survive. He was 16 years old at the time. He did not expect to live beyond about age 25. I wonder now if he is still among the living.

Reminder 11:

Pride and power can get in the way of your forgiving. They can get in the way of positively transforming who you are as a person.

Let us strengthen what we have just learned about pride and power with a series of exercises. Five exercises follow here, but of course you need not go through them at one sitting. It is far preferable to go through them thoroughly and leisurely. The learning needs to sink into you deeply and abide in you, hopefully for the rest of your life. After this workout, I think that you will feel stronger to enter the next door with our third key. So, with this overview in mind, let's begin.

Exercise #3: Build Your Forgiveness Muscles: How Your Understanding of Forgiveness Is Shaped by the Lens of Power or the Lens of Love

It's time to glean important insights into how your views of power and love influence your understanding of forgiveness. As you will see, the differences between these two are stark. For now, please look through the lens of power as I make the following statements and you consider how you would answer me as one who sees through the power lens.

• Forgiveness is for weaklings. If you cannot take the advantage from someone, then you lie down and forgive. Through your power lens, does this sound about right?

- When I forgive, I am simply making excuses for some-one's bad behavior because I do not have the guts to con-front him or her. Reasonable?
- Forgive and never forget. Pretend to forgive . . . and then get even.
- Unless the other is willing to give me something in re-turn, I will never reconcile with that person. I have a list and I regularly cross people off of that list. Doesn't this make sense when seen through the power lens?
- Not all persons are equal. Some are sheep. Sheep are meant to be sheared.

Look at each statement again, now in the form of a question, through the eyes of clearer vision, service love, and mercy. Con-sider your answers through the new lens of love.

- Is forgiveness for weaklings? No. To give of oneself in service to others and to stand firm in that is an act of great strength.
- Is forgiveness a veiled excuse to avoid confrontation? No. To lie down and cringe in the face of another's cruelty is not to help him or her at all. When I forgive, I am doing so, in conjunction with justice, for that other person's good. He or she needs correc-tion, but a correction that does not take a pound of flesh from him or her.
- Is forgiveness a game of pretend to gain an advantage? If it is, then I am playing the game not only on that person but also on myself. I am being unfaithful to who I am as a person and to whom I know the other to be—a person who is special, unique, and irreplaceable in this world. I am doing harm to both of us with that worldview.
- Is it okay to regularly cross people off of my list of who is human? No. People are not to be "crossed off." You might not reconcile with another, but you do not cross that person off your list of all who are human beings. Why not? You can answer this one for yourself.
- Are some people sheep? This is such a demeaning com-

ment that it likely hurts the humanity of the one who holds such a thought. The statement implies that people are to be used for others' ends.

Reminder 12:

Power and love vie for your attention.

One might even say that power and love are in a power struggle for your very humanity and for the humanity of those around you and for those who hurt you. As you see the world from the position of power, you are likely to develop not only a skepticism about forgiveness but also an annoyance or even a hatred toward it. As you view the world from the position of love, in contrast, you develop a deep appreciation that forgiveness is a way to mend the cracks and breaks in hearts, relationships, and communities. Forgiveness binds together in love. Power has the potential to separate and destroy.

As you move through the journey of your life, you will encounter people who have a predominant worldview of power. Those may be the ones who have wounded you, sometimes over and over again. All of us may hold some combination of these two worldviews, but as you pay very close attention, you will see that the scales for all of us tip one way or the other, in the direction of love or power.

Exercise #4: Build Your Forgiveness Muscles: Seeing Power in the World

The purpose of this exercise is to help you train your mind to become much sharper in seeing power where it exists in the world, so that you do not inadvertently drift into joining those who have this worldview. It is quite easy to do that: to just drift almost unconsciously into picking up the power lens and then treating people as objects for your own ends because so many around you are doing this. The point here, though, is not to become so hypervigilant and imbalanced that you begin to see power where no power is being exerted. So it's important to maintain balance and reason when doing this exercise. Where there is power, it is important to see it and to stand in the strength of your vision to label it as it is: an expression of power. This exercise also should help you identify people who are being unjust toward you as you now recognize how their worldview is influencing their actions. Now to the exercise.

Make a list of at least five instances in the world today, or specifically in your community, in which people operated with pride and power and not with clearer vision, love, or mercy. Here are two examples to get you started: This first one happened to me lately. A person who knows how to hack credit cards stole my credit card information. As a first test, the person used my card to sign me up for a travel magazine and quickly followed with an attempt to purchase $3,000 of scuba diving equipment. The magazine effort as the first wave of the theft was clever because it left a travel trail for the security department of my credit card company. The person made it look like I was interested in travel and so the big purchase of the scuba equipment might seem like a rational second step. It did not work because of the sharper minds in the security department. The person used his or her creativity to try to take advantage of me, to exert power over me.

As the second example, some of you may remember an American company, Enron, that claimed to be such an energy giant that it supposedly amassed $101 billion in 2000. As it turned out, the company executives were cooking their books and lying about how powerful they were—to become more powerful. We talk of the company in the past tense because it folded . . . over the quest for power. As you can see, this power grab was not some kind of one-time weakness but an ongoing, deliberate,

and cultivated way of living. The company chose decep-
tion, fraud, and thievery to gain power over others—a
very far cry from service.

Now it's your turn to list five examples of power over
love. Think of political figures, bosses, drivers on your high-
ways, people in authority, and acquaintances. Look at television commercials and ads online or in newspapers. What
is the subtle message in many of them? Then ask yourself
this question: *How common is this worldview of power in
the world today and in my own community?* As we will see
in the next chapter, you likely have been hurt, and perhaps
deeply, by people who hold a worldview based on pride
and power.

Exercise #5: Build Your Forgiveness Muscles: Seeing the Extent to Which You Operate from a Power Worldview

This next exercise explores *your* worldview. Have you been
operating, perhaps without even realizing it, from a worldview of pride and power? I ask this question because if you
choose to train your mind toward forgiveness, it is necessary to see the very subtle, almost hidden foes that may
weaken your efforts. And how might pride and power
weaken your efforts to forgive? By making you feel entitled,
inflated, so deserving that you will hang onto your resentment as a noble cause—in the name of pride and power
that are so subtle that you will not even call them by their
right names when you see them.

Here is one example. Helen was a churchgoer who
wanted others to see her as a good religious woman. She
smiled broadly, was helpful to others who asked for her aid,
and was always quick with an assuring, "I forgive you."
Everyone loved Helen. Yet, deep inside of her, she harbored thoughts of power. First of all, she wanted to be
admired for her apparently cheerful approach to life. Deep
down she would sulk about even small slights to herself,
and she raged inside about deep injustices that would

come her way. No one ever saw this because she kept these hidden in her heart. Her outer expression suggested that she operated from a worldview of love. Her inner reality belied this. She was unhappy, resentful, and kept up the good front because of pride. She wanted to be loved. Her loving demeanor was actually a quest for power by using the appearance of love to achieve her goal. She was miserable inside and eventually sought therapy for psychological depression. Her worldview of pride and power was making her sick.

So, with this introduction in mind, list five ways that you have exercised pride and power when you could have been exercising clearer vision, love, and mercy. The point is not to embarrass you or to judge you poorly. Any person embarking on this forgiveness journey must also examine his or her own worldview very thoroughly to learn how to detect subtle clues that he or she is operating from a power worldview. Ask yourself these questions:

- How common is this worldview within me?
- How happy am I as a person when I look through the lens of power and act on this vision?

You might keep a log for a week and jot down instances in which you catch yourself acting from a power worldview. You can refer to Helen's experience as an example to guide your reflections. Of course, your experiences may not be as dramatic as Helen's, so please just see hers as a general example for you.

Exercises to Increase Your Fitness in Love, Mercy, and Forgiveness

Now that you have been introduced to love and mercy and their opponents, pride and power, let's begin developing the life-giving qualities of love, mercy, and forgiveness through the next two exercises.

Exercise #6: Build Your Forgiveness Muscles: Training Your Mind to See Clearer Vision, Service Love, and Mercy in the World

Because this exercise is specifically intended to strengthen your use of the love lens as a worldview, it is not about *doing*, but about *seeing*. The purpose is to train your mind to see love in the world in general (as you worked to see power in the world in Exercise #4). This is not about asking you to change your approach to the world yet. That will come later. For now, just begin shifting your focus—your thoughts and attention—away from power and toward the "Big Three" of clearer vision, service love, and mercy. Once you *see* these, we will then work on your *doing* them in Exercise 7, and eventually, to applying all of this to your forgiving others with Keys 4 and 8.

Your task in this exercise is to begin seeing the Big Three as they are being expressed by others anywhere in the world. Look through a newspaper (whether online or delivered to your door) to find one example—just one—of people going beyond the ordinary to *see* others as persons who are special, unique, and irreplaceable. One of the really good things about our global network these days is that acts of kindness "go viral" just as the tragedies and atrocities do. YouTube is filled with these "goodies." With such resources, it shouldn't be difficult to find one person who has demonstrated the Big Three and to reflect on his or her actions for a few minutes.

I did this exercise this morning and thought about a story that went viral on the Internet. It was a photo of an African-American man sleeping on a subway car. He was resting his head on a Jewish man's shoulder. The Jewish man, wearing a yarmulke, was simply letting the man rest on him, explaining that he realized the sleeping man was tired and needed some rest. He was using clearer vision in understanding the sleeping man as a person, who should be respected and cared for. This example shows both clearer vision and service love blended together.

Now try to find or think of a story in which someone is demonstrating service love to others. The story above about the Amish is an excellent example of service love. Try to find your own example so that you are engaging actively in this exercise rather than only reading my examples. Active engagement is really the only way to strengthen your worldview toward service love.

Finally, seek out a story of mercy in the world. There are many of these on the International Forgiveness Institute's website (www.internationalforgiveness.com) in the Forgiveness News section. There you will find people from all over the world reaching out to others who have gravely wounded them. These stories lift one's spirit as we all share in the bravery and love of those who have been wounded.

Exercise #7: Build Your Forgiveness Muscles: Practicing Clearer Vision and Service Love Today

It's time to add the dimension of *doing* to your *seeing*. This exercise is particularly important for cultivating the habit of bringing the Big Three into your everyday world. We will hold off on the mercy side of things for now because it is not yet time to do the forgiving, which will come in Key 4. For now, focus on nurturing clearer vision when you are with others today.

For this exercise first choose five people on whom to focus. They need not all be people with whom you interact. For example, one person might be someone whom you pass on the street. Others should be people with whom you are in direct contact either physically or by Internet interactions. Say the following statements to yourself—to *yourself*, not to the person directly:

- "This person is special, unique, and irreplaceable in this world."
- "This person may likely have been wounded in the past. He or she is carrying those wounds silently in his or her heart today."
- "This person may already have encountered some injustice today and could be hurting because of this."

Three statements for five people. You might want to write them out and hang them on a wall or with a magnet on the refrigerator. Keep the statements before you so you can remember to state them to yourself. Even memorize them if that's easy for you to do.

As the second part of this exercise, your task is to demonstrate service love in some way to at least five people today. A hug, a smile, a "like" on a social media website; being patient with a cashier who is tired; showing understanding to a hurting colleague; comforting a child; adding a cheerful and encouraging ending to an online correspondence; making a modest contribution to a charity—all of these are expressions of service love.

Reminder 13:

You can practice clearer vision and service love toward other people whenever you want.

Principle 5: Practice Forgiveness Itself in Small Ways Each Day

When you are learning to forgive, it is often best to take small steps at first. In this way you build confidence as you become more familiar and comfortable with it. In that spirit, let's start with a small forgiveness exercise: to become aware of the little aggravations you experience today and then to forgive those people who are aggravating you. Please remember from Key 1 that you only forgive persons and not inanimate objects.

Exercise #8: Build Your Forgiveness Muscles: Practicing Clearer Vision, Service Love, and Mercy in the Context of Minor Aggravations Today

This exercise brings us closer to forgiveness by centering on minor annoyances that we face daily: a colleague who is late for a meeting, a child who is tired and not listening well to your requests, waiting in a long line for the cashier. All of these are opportunities to engage in this exercise.

Your task today is to find one person toward whom you can practice the Big Three. As you find this person who is annoying you in a minor way, first repeat to yourself the three (possibly memorized) statements. Here are their short versions again as tips: "This person is special; he or she has been hurt in the past; he or she may be struggling with an injustice that I did not see happen."

Next, practice service love in actual behavior. Even in your annoyance, as you see this individual as a special person (because we all are), try to express this realization in some concrete way (a smile, a sympathetic word) and practice merciful restraint (so that you do not retaliate in your frustration). Try to lift the person up, gently, simply because you are there and are able to do this.

This exercise is for today and it is for *every* day because it is a powerful (in the morally good sense of this term) way to strengthen the worldview of love in you.

Reminder 14:

You can respond to minor annoyances with the Big Three of clearer vision, service love, and mercy.

Principle 6: Practice Being Consistent in Your Forgiveness

Our feelings sometimes get in the way of our willingness and ability to forgive. When we are very angry, we are in no mood to forgive. When the act is more of an annoyance than a serious offense, it is much easier to offer forgiveness through the practice of the Big Three.

The challenge now is to try to make your commitment to forgive as consistent as possible even when you are not feeling like it or your anger is getting in the way. I'm not suggesting that you have to forgive immediately. Instead, I'm challenging you to become so forgivingly fit that your clearer vision becomes more like a habit. By this I mean that you just begin to see people through this lens, no matter who this person is, no matter what your inner circumstances are, or what the actions from the other are.

Exercise #9: Build Your Forgiveness Muscles: Being Consistent in Practicing Forgiveness Across Different Situations

Here are three scenarios for you to imagine as a way to practice being consistent in your forgiving. In each case, try to be consistent in your offer of forgiveness.

- *Scenario 1.* You are very tired, on your way home in the evening, and someone cuts you off in traffic. You have to slam on your brakes and your heart starts to beat faster because of the near accident. Can you see the person as special, unique, and irreplaceable despite this? Are you willing to commit to forgiving, even if it comes later?
- *Scenario 2.* One of your loved ones needs your attention, but you are not feeling well. In fact, you find that he or she is almost demanding of you when you have little left to give. You find yourself getting angry inside. Are you willing to check that anger so it does not come pouring out in an unhealthy way? Are you willing to start a forgiveness exercise with the Big Three so that your anger does not get the

better of you, either inside or out? Please do not see this as a grim obligation but instead as a way to help toward your emotional well-being.

- *Scenario 3.* The phone rings and you are very busy. You look at the Caller ID quickly and think it is from a friend. Once you pick up the phone, you are greeted by a telemarketer. Are you willing to *do no harm* by refraining from slamming the phone down or being impolite? Are you willing to immediately begin to see that this person is special, unique, and irreplaceable and to respond in kind to that insight?

Forgiveness is starting to be a part of your life if you can maintain a forgiving stance in the face of these three rather different and not so atypical situations. Your practice in one of them may generalize to others and help you in real-life situations that call for mercy rather than anger. The key point is to practice forgiveness like this every day.

Principle 7: Persevere in Your Practice of Forgiveness Each Day

As I mentioned earlier in the book, I have been studying forgiveness since the mid-1980s. In that time I have learned this: Many people get quite excited about forgiveness at first and just dive into practicing it, only to lose interest after a few months. They literally just let it fade from their minds and hearts as they go on to the next popular diversion in life. They do not have a strong will to keep forgiveness alive within them as a practice and as a way of seeing the world.

This could happen to you. A commitment to forgive does not just mean a short-term commitment toward one person who has hurt you in one particular way. *Commitment* has a must longer reach than this. Would you become physically fit if you worked out several times a week for three months and then hung it all up?

Of course, not. It is the same with forgiveness. You have to fight against the tendency to just let it fade in you. You will have to fight against all of the distractions of life that call you away from it.

Reminder 15:

Forgiveness can fade in you to where you no longer even think about it. Do yourself and others a favor by not letting that happen.

Exercise #10: Build Your Forgiveness Muscles by Persisting in Your Practice of Forgiveness

Following are five questions to help you persevere in the practice of forgiveness for the rest of your life.

- Are you aware that forgiveness could easily fade in you?
- Who might you partner with as a "forgiveness workout buddy" so that you can help each other keep up the work of forgiveness for your and your buddy's health and the well-being of others who could be the recipients of either of your unhealthy anger?
- What are some of the major diversions that perhaps lull you into submission as you let forgiveness fade in you? Name them and be aware of them. These are the foes of your well-being.
- Can you set aside three minutes each day to review your forgiveness progress? Just three minutes. If that proves to be too much, can you give it two minutes . . . every day?
- Are you aware of the benefits to forgiving? Review those occasionally as motivation to keep going in this process of becoming forgivingly fit.

> **Reminder 16:**
> Persevering in your forgiveness practice may be one of your greatest and most rewarding challenges throughout your life.

Toward the Future

The exercises for Key 2 are meant to strengthen your view of and interaction with people in a general way so that you will be ready for the rigors of forgiving those who have deeply hurt you. Equipping yourself with these new ways of seeing and interacting in the world, as described here, will be applied to how you forgive using Keys 4–8. This is why you need to keep practicing the material in this chapter, so that it becomes more natural for you. It would be quite easy to just put all of the learning here aside as you strive for healing from your specific emotional wounds, but please keep in mind that this foundation may form the basis of even deeper healing for you. Working on the material in this Key 2 so that it becomes a part of your forgiveness habit in your everyday life will make the remaining steps in your forgiveness journey possible.

IDENTIFY THE SOURCE OF YOUR PAIN AND ADDRESS YOUR INNER TURMOIL

Yes, I am carrying pain in my heart today because of others' unjust treatment of me. This pain is not forever. There are proven ways to overcome that pain, and forgiveness is one scientifically supported way for me to do that. I choose to heal so that the psychological effects of the other's power over me vanish.

We have arrived at our third door, holding our third key. Here, please take the key and open this one yourself. I ask because this is a hard one and I want you to show your courage and commitment to work on your wounds by opening this door and walking in first. I want you to see that you can and will stand before the pain, see it for what it is, and not be defeated by it. Your opening this door is the first step in this emotional healing. So, when you are ready, please lead me into this room of pain. And let us remember this: There is an exit to this room. We will not be in here forever. The exit is into the sunshine, a state you may not have experienced for a long time. It is out there waiting for us and we will be going out soon. So, I am with you and we will get through this together.

Reminder 17:

There is healing for your pain through the practice of forgiveness if you choose to be healed.

Understanding Injustices and
Their Consequences

When you choose a person to forgive, you want to be sure that he or she truly was unjust to you. For example, Kari was very angry with her boss for not showing up to an important meeting. When the meeting was over, she had a message waiting for her. It was from her boss. He apologized for his absence. His daughter was in an accident and he had to rush her to the hospital with no time to call the office. Kari realized that her boss had a stronger obligation to his daughter than he had to the employees in the company under the circumstances. The boss did not commit an offense in need of forgiveness. We have to take the time to examine when there is a person deserving your time and attention to forgive and when forgiveness is unnecessary because no offense was committed in the first place.

An *injustice* is any action or inaction (such as deliberately missing a meeting without a good excuse) that is directed at you by a person and that you do not deserve. *By a person* is an important phrase because it confines the focus to people; tornadoes and other acts of nature are not persons and so cannot act unjustly toward you. Sometimes that person is you, yourself, as we will see in Key 7. Injustices are failures to meet obligations. Here is what I mean. To be able to live well on this planet all people need to have access to these basic rights: the right to clean air to breathe, the right to food that will nourish, the right to protection from harsh weather, the right to be treated as a human being. Because you have rights, others have obligations not to block those rights. Either deliberately or through unthinking neglect, a person is unjust to you whenever he or she blocks your legitimate rights.

Someone who steals from you has an obligation not to do that. This is a deliberate violation of your right to your own property. But what if you have 1,000 loaves of bread and your neighbor has none? Then it is your obligation to be just, not the other's right to force that obligation upon you.

Reminder 18:

We all have rights and obligations. Those who pull away your rights are being unjust.

Sometimes the injustice is not a deliberate act, as is stealing what belongs to you. Suppose you are driving in your car and a driver runs a red light and hits you broadside, totaling your car and your knee. "But I did not do this deliberately!" is the offending driver's cry. So what? He had an obligation to be paying attention because of the dire consequences that could happen and did happen to you. You have a right to a functioning car and knee.

Reminder 19:

Obligations can be broken deliberately or passively without the person intending it. In either case, a broken obligation damages your rights.

So often, broken obligations and assaults on your basic rights involve the other's use of power over you (I again am using the word *power* in its negative sense). It is a clash within the other's inner world, a distortion of what the person thinks are his or her rights and what he or she fails to see as your rights.

> "But I had to text that person while I was driving."
> "He had it coming. He made me mad."
> "She had it coming. She insulted me."

An eye-for-an-eye is not always just, you see. If you are unjust to others, they do not have a right to be unjust back. They have an obligation to meet your injustice with justice. This can be done by a verbal correction, for example, if you treated the person with disrespect.

Do not be persuaded that an injustice is not an injustice when a person using power tells you that you are wrong, you were not treated unjustly. "You are mistaken," they will proclaim. "Get a life," they will say with disdain. "Get over it," they will whisper with indifference. This is a power play.

Reminder 20:

The other's worldview of power can result in injustices toward you in the false name of goodness. Don't be fooled by his or her argument that you were not treated unjustly.

At the same time, be on guard against interpreting everything through the lens of power because then you see injustices at every turn where there are none. Here are some examples of false perceptions of injustice:

> "My instructor at the university has no right to give me homework because I lead a busy life."
> "My partner has no right to down time when I'm ready to go out on the town."
> "My children have no right to be imperfect."
> "No one has the right to correct me even if I did wrong."

You can distort your own obligations and the other's rights if you are not careful.

Reminder 21:

When you use the lens of power, you distort what is and what is not an injustice against you. You can too easily accuse others of injustices that are not injustices. Shed the lens of power to have clearer vision.

Finally, we must realize that there are true injustices through truly broken obligations that hurt your genuine rights. When your rights are damaged, you hurt. Injustices toward you have consequences that can hurt you as much as, or even more than, the harm done at the point the injustice happened. We have to work on these effects of injustice for your own good. You can feel very disrupted inside, very unsettled, sad, and confused—a state of inner turmoil.

Reminder 22:

When someone is unjust to you, the consequences can be very damaging for you. You have a right to fix those consequences, especially those internal consequences that I call *inner turmoil*.

Because you hurt when the other is unjust toward you, you have a right to healing. That is where we are headed in Key 4. In this chapter let's take time to identify the source of your pain in a general way, because you are likely not a doctor, counselor, or health care worker who can professionally diagnose your precise issue of inner turmoil. I am talking here in more general terms, which all people do, for example, before they seek medical help. Surely, you know that your knee is hurting in a big way when you go to the emergency room. You first make a kind of preliminary diagnosis that something definitely is not right. That is the point here: For you to make a kind of initial diagnosis of your inner world so that you can proceed toward the best remedy for you. Shall we begin to look at your inner world as it is right now toward the important goal of that healing for you? Let me repeat: You have the right to being emotionally healed from others' unjust actions. As we proceed it is important to see that we are not judging or condemning persons. Instead, we are examining actions and calling them unjust when this is the case.

Figuring Out Which People to Forgive and in Which Order

Before beginning to figure out on whom to focus in your forgiveness journey, listen to the following stories of hurt as a way to help you see some of the subtle ways in which you may be carrying your internal wounds from injustices that have happened in the past or are happening now. The point here is not to take on the hurts of others as your own. Instead, use these examples to ask these two questions: "Who hurt me?" and "Who hurt me the most?" These are the ones for whom you will be going on this forgiveness journey in the next chapter . . . for the good of the other (because forgiveness is about goodness) and for the healing of your inner world (because you have a right to this healing).

Not all of these stories will be directly relevant to you. Some, however, may be very relevant because, perhaps, you had not thought about your own situation in quite this way before. In either case, these stories are intended to help you gain insight into your inner world.

The Father Wound and Peer Wounds

Christopher is a middle school teacher, a career he has had for 10 years. The students can't stand him. He is authoritarian, bordering on rude. He assigns so much work that the students feel choked by it all. Because he demands respect, the students do not challenge his way in the classroom. Instead they suffer through it and wish they were never assigned to his class. No one is happy, including Christopher.

As a child, he was not good in sports and at times his peers would mock him so that he felt quite apart from them. He secretly yearned to be part of the peer group, but he never quite fit in. His father was a demanding man, expecting high standards of behavior and achievement in school. Christopher felt that he was never quite accepted by his own father because he was always falling just a little short of his father's expectations. Christopher grew up frustrated, unfulfilled, and angry—but he did not realize that he was angry. After all, he had to rely on his father when he was a child, and he had no choice regarding who his peers were in school. So, he just stuffed down the anger by denying it.

Yet it did exist and still does. What he did not get from his peers while growing up—respect—he now demanded from his students. He copied his father's high standards and imposed them on each of his students. Misery begot misery, which produced even more misery. Christopher was wounded and until he could finally realize this, he was trapped and kept many a student trapped in his room of resentment. He exercised power over an age group that had exerted power over him years ago, and he did it through an authoritarian stance that mirrored his father's attitude toward him when he was a child. Christopher was reproducing his wounds by imposing them on others. Were he to start forgiveness therapy, Christopher's primary wound would be recognized as coming from his father, who had severely damaged his son's self-image. Christopher's peers then inflicted his secondary wounds. Unless he forgives his father, Christopher's lingering anger could get in the way of his forgiving the peers, if he decided to forgive the peers first. So the best route for Christopher would be to forgive his father and then the peers, in that order.

The Mother Wound and the Partner Wound

Samantha was the oldest of three children. Her depressed mother had had little energy to clean the house, prepare good meals, or attend to her children's physical and psychological needs. As a result, Samantha did not form a strong bond of attachment with her mother. The attachment bond that forms in early childhood when good parenting is available is vital to develop trust in others. As a young adult, Samantha's weak sense of trust got in the way of her dating. She could not allow herself to get emotionally close to any potential partner. She failed at five different relationship attempts. In two of these relationships, Samantha's lack of a healthy attachment with her mother led her to make poor choices in her partners. One of the partners had a severe problem with alcohol. Samantha did not even see this at first and when she eventually did, she thought that she could somehow help "fix" the situation. In the other problem relationship, the person was verbally abusive. She again thought that with time, the abuse would end.

As a result of these five failed relationships, she remained single all her adult life. She did not have a close circle of friends and found her solace in her career. She was lonely and angry. She blamed the partners for her troubled state, focusing on little flaws (in three cases) and the considerable flaws (in the two cases), so that she could justify the fact that none of the romantic attempts had worked out. Her worldview became quite negative, and she concluded that partnering is a self-interested and selfish undertaking in which she wanted no part. Her loneliness gave way to major depression. When she sought help, her therapist held the worldview that depression is primarily biological and so treated her symptoms without ever unearthing the issues of poor attachment, mistrust, anger, and the need to forgive her mother for failing to establish that all-important attachment bond. Although the therapist did focus on the two partners whose behavior was extreme, he failed to go back far enough to the mother.

Had Samantha entered forgiveness therapy, she would have addressed issues with her mother (primary wound) and with at least two of the partners (secondary wounds). Her central person to forgive is her mother. Even if she started forgiveness therapy by trying to forgive, say, the verbally abusive person, she still would have had to make her way to her mother, who had done the most serious wounding by failing to form a healthy attachment with her daughter. Without forgiving her mother, Samantha might find it hard to reach out in mercy to others because her trust was so damaged in early childhood.

The Ethnic/Racial Wound and Wounds from a Particular Group

Janice had just relocated from the Philippines to a mid-sized city in Western Europe with her husband, James, and their son, Rodrigo. Once settled in the new city, she began noticing what she described as an "unfriendly attitude" from some people, even those she did not know. When she and James looked into this, they discovered that there had been tension in the city because within the past two years, nurses from Thailand were answering ads to come to this city to staff hospitals in which there was a nursing shortage. It became apparent to them that too many residents failed to realize that the hospitals were the ones recruiting. It was not as if nurses in Thailand just decided to immigrate and flood this particular city. Nevertheless, some of the citizens wrongfully assumed that those from Thailand were taking jobs away from the locals. And Janice was not even from Thailand.

Janice and James were now stuck in an unhealthy situation. They were continually feeling a general negative response to them when in public, and Janice was growing resentful. At the same time, Rodrigo was experiencing some alienation in school from a small group of students, and she was worried. The vast majority of people in the wider community and in Rodrigo's school reacted civilly, but the incivility happened enough so that she felt as if her family's quality of life was compromised.

She now sees an ethnic bias that is a norm, at least for some, which is hard to break. Because of this norm, she senses subtle condemnation of her as a person just because she is who she is. It wounds her heart.

Janice is constantly fighting an inner anger that she identifies as unhealthy, brought on by a kind of helpless feeling that this issue of ethnic bias is not going away any time soon. The feeling of being trapped increases her anger, which has lately turned into anxiety as well.

If Janice were to start forgiveness therapy, her primary wound would be identified as coming from the larger society through the perpetuation of subtle and not-so-subtle forms of ethnic stereotyping and bias. How can one forgive norms? Norms are not people, and we can forgive people, not inanimate objects and abstract ideas. Janice would not be forgiving the norms but the people who hold and perpetuate the norms. It is possible to forgive groups, even large, abstract groups such as society. We address this theme in the next chapter. Janice's secondary wounds are from the handful of students at Rodrigo's school.

Janice's ongoing pain from the wounds caused by ethnic bias

may be spilling over to other areas of her life, for example, in her correspondence with her parents back in the Philippines. Lately she has been corresponding less because she does not want to share her experiences with her parents, who likely would begin to worry. Forgiving those who perpetuate such norms may quiet her inner world enough to then do the forgiveness work toward those who bring these norms concretely into her son's school.

Before the focus shifts to identifying your sources of injustice and woundedness, let's pause and consider a new idea in the area of psychotherapy so that you are protected.

Before Identifying the People Who Wounded You: A Note on Retraumatization

As I write this, there is a school of thought within psychotherapy that says this: Do not ask a client to revisit the traumatic events as they unfolded for him or her. There is no need to open the wound yet again as he or she moves forward in life. Identify the adaptive ways the client can use now to move further away from that trauma. If you go back in time to do this revisiting, you are delaying the trip toward greater wholeness.

The advice is good to a point. As an example, suppose someone comes to an orthopedic surgeon because of an injured shoulder caused by a serious car accident. If the doctor spends a lot of time asking about the details of the car accident, this focus could induce anxiety in the patient. Suppose the surgeon dwells on the little details of what happened as the patient saw the other car coming at her, what her reaction was at impact, and what her psychological state was once she was hit. None of her answers to these inappropriate questions could possibly repair the shoulder. This kind of inquiry is more than just wasted time. It might retraumatize the patient without playing any part whatsoever in the healing of her shoulder. What is needed now is a diagnosis of that shoulder.

Part of the diagnosis is knowing how the injury happened. Was the person reaching for a jar in her home and all of a sudden the shoulder became excruciatingly painful? Was there an accident? A fall? It is important for the doctor to know if this injury was from a traumatic event or from wear-and-tear over time, now revealed by the simple act of reaching for a jar. Knowing the "how" will help with knowing the treatment strategy. (A wear-and-tear rotator cuff injury, for example, may be harder to fix through surgery than a recent traumatic blow to the shoulder.)

Part of that diagnosis requires figuring out what the patient's shoulder can and cannot do right now. This will involve some exercises, or attempted exercises, such as raising the arm to the front and then raising it from the side. The diagnosis may involve the painful activity of raising the arm while a professional puts some resistance on that arm, and that can hurt.

Do you see that there is a substantial difference between revisiting the details of an event itself and examining the "how" of the event and its aftereffects? Asking the patient what the context was when the shoulder was injured and identifying the aftereffects by testing the arm's strength and range of movement are not the same as a detailed revisiting of the car accident. Yes, there could be some emotional trauma from the diagnostic procedure, from explaining that it was a car accident, from the surgery itself (if needed), and from the rehabilitation over the coming months. Yet none of these can be classified as retraumatizing the patient. The doctor is assessing the basics of what needs to be assessed.

With the exercises we will be doing now, you will not need to revisit the precise details of what happened to you in any explicit way. You will be asked to identify the injustice you experienced. After all, whom will you know to forgive if you cannot connect an injustice with a person or persons? It is equally important to examine the aftereffects, the consequences for you of how the other treated you, so that we can discern whether or not this person is vital to forgive (from a psychological viewpoint) or not. If you were only mildly wounded by a certain person, let's move on to another who hurt you deeply enough that you need the heart surgery of forgiveness.

This step is necessary to identify the kind of care you will need. As in the case of the surgeon and the shoulder, you may end up needing less care than you might think. On the other hand, if the symptoms of injury are severe, you definitely should continue with the rehabilitation of your heart so that the symptoms lessen and the cause of those symptoms can be directly addressed.

As one more important point: Because forgiveness is a moral virtue, it is always good to forgive anyone who has been unjust to you whether or not you have been deeply hurt or not. Why? Because goodness is worth practicing anywhere and any time just because it is good.

Reminder 23:

Forgiveness is good in and of itself.

Reminder 24:

From a psychological perspective, forgiveness is a good practice in which to engage because it can heal the person who was wounded. This does not make forgiveness a self-serving activity when we focus on the consequences of injustice and want to heal from them.

Identifying the People Who May Have Hurt You

If you are to know whom to forgive, you have to examine the people in your life from childhood to the present. I know that is a long sweep of time, but you really do need to take a look so that you can carefully choose the people who have damaged your heart.

Let's now look at some of the categories of people who may have done the wounding. This is not an exhaustive list, just a starting point. Add to it as you recall those who have wounded you who are not suggested here.

Exercise #1: Who Hurt You?

Your task in this exercise is to simply *record your answers* to these questions in the context of the material that follows, in which the categories of father, mother, siblings, peers, teachers, partner(s), employers/coworkers, your own children, yourself, your community, and your ethnicity, race, and other forms of prejudice are described:

  I. Did this person act unjustly toward me, perhaps by exercising power over me or by withdrawing love from me? Yes or no?

 II. If so, how serious was the injustice or pattern of injustice (was the behavior a habit for this person)? You can give each person a rating:
    1. Mild
    2. Somewhat hurtful
    3. Hurtful
    4. Very hurtful
    5. Extremely hurtful

III. When you consider all of your inner pain, to what degree has this person contributed to that pain? You can rate the person this way:
    1. To a very minimal degree
    2. To a small degree
    3. To a degree
    4. To a large degree
    5. To an enormous degree

Father

Were you hurt by your father? Fathers have a way of damaging confidence when power is involved. Your father's actions can affect your adult relationships with men such as damaging trust, making friendships difficult. Your father's actions can have an effect on your spiritual or religious life, especially if your religion includes the image of God as Father. Without dwelling on it, please name the injustice or the pattern of injustice that you experienced. You can forgive someone for a general trend of unfairness when there are too many individual incidents to count. How hurtful was this act or series of acts by your father? Do you think that what you experienced with your father has negatively affected your inner world?

Mother

Answer the same three questions: Were you hurt by your mother? How hurtful was this act or series of acts by your mother? Do you think that what you experienced with your mother has negatively affected your inner world? As we have seen in the case studies, mothers can damage trust when there is a failure to nurture a healthy attachment with the young child. This basic failure can lead to difficulties in establishing loving relationships as an adult.

Siblings

If more than one sibling has hurt you, name each and answer the three questions for each:

Were you hurt by [name of sibling]? How hurtful was this act or series of acts by [name of sibling]? Do you think that what you experienced with [name of sibling] has negatively affected your inner world? The sibling wound can contribute to conflict in adult relationships. Look at the story of Joseph as some insight here for you.

Peers

Peers can engage in bullying, which can harm our self-image and our self-respect. This wounded self-image can be carried into adulthood. Recall our case study above in which Christopher tried to compensate, for his entire adult life until he entered therapy, for peer criticism experienced when he was young.

If more than one peer has hurt you, name each and answer the three questions for each: Were you hurt by [name of peer]? How hurtful was this act or series of acts by [name of peer]? Do you think that what you experienced with [name of peer] has negatively affected your inner world?

Teachers

Teachers who hurt their students tend to wound their self-image as learners. These young people begin to think, in the back of their minds, "I'm stupid," "I'm bad," "I'm uncooperative." If this rings a bell for you, ask yourself, "Am I *really* . . . stupid, or bad, or uncooperative?" Key 4 addresses problems with self-image based on these kinds of experiences. For now, answer the three questions for teachers and all others connected with your educational experiences (coaches, for example): Were you hurt by [name of teacher/principal/coach]? How hurtful was this act or series of acts by [name of teacher/principal/coach]? Do you think that what you experienced with [name of teacher/principal/coach] has negatively affected your inner world?

Partner(s)

We tend to be most hurt by those who have committed to give us love but have betrayed that love. Sometimes that person was affected by his or her mother or father wound and passes on that injury. Sometimes you are the one who was (and continues to be) affected by your mother or father wound. So the hurt is an extension of a prior wound, perhaps from childhood. Consider any partner who may have been unjust, hurt you deeply, and is contributing now to your inner turmoil: Were you hurt by [name of partner]? How hurtful was this act or series of acts by [name of partner]? Do you think that what you experienced with [name of partner] has negatively affected your inner world?

Employers/Coworkers

Too often the workplace is fertile ground for the exertion of power—and power exerted toward you hurts. An authoritarian employer may have a father wound that was passed to you. Of course, not all bossy bosses have father wounds, but this surely is one avenue toward bringing hurtful power into the workplace. Sometimes coworkers can be under much stress and act insensitively toward others. Were you hurt by [name of employer/coworker]? How hurtful was this act or series of acts by [name of employer/coworker]? Do you think that what you experienced with [name of employer/coworker] has negatively affected your inner world?

Your Own Children

Children have a way of growing up with their own wounds and then passing them to the older generation. A wound from the schoolyard, or a teacher, or an employer, or one of you as the parents can contribute to unjust actions by your own child. It takes courage to look at this one and answer truthfully: Yes, my son/daughter hurt me. So, with courage in hand, answer the three questions about your own child or children: Were you hurt by [name of child]? How hurtful was this act or series of acts by [name of child]? Do you think that what you experienced with [name of child] has negatively affected your inner world?

Yourself

Yes, you can hurt yourself. I will be saying a lot about this point in a detailed examination in Key 7. For now, fill out the three questions with regard to yourself as the one who has hurt you. Did you hurt yourself? How hurtful was this act or series of acts against yourself? Do you think that what you experienced by your own thoughts and actions has negatively affected your inner world?

Your Community

We belong to many communities: local neighborhoods, our cities, and houses of worship are all examples. Have there been certain attitudes by people in one of your communities that have been unjust, led to hurt, and perhaps contributed to your inner stress? Find out by rating your various communities for the three questions: Were you hurt by [name of community]? How hurtful was this act or series of acts by [name of community]? Do you think that what you experienced with [name of community] has negatively affected your inner world?

Your Ethnicity, Race, and Other Forms of Prejudice

In Janice's case study we saw how norms in society have a way of communicating a harsh and undeserved message to many. You may be one of those who has suffered in this way. If so, examine the extent of this injury by answering the three questions with regard to your society and your experience within it. This is a tougher area to evaluate because there is not one particular person looking at you with angry eyes. Yet, you know when such norms exist, so if you have felt this form of hurt, rate the three questions in relation to the societal prejudice you have experienced: Were you hurt by [type of societal prejudice]? How hurtful was this act or series of acts by [type of societal prejudice]? Do you think that what you experienced with [type of societal prejudice] has negatively affected your inner world?

Any Others Not Listed Here

Who else hurt you? List them now, even if you do not know the person's name. Maybe you were the victim of a home break-in or armed robbery. You can see that person in your mind's eye, even if you cannot put a name or even a clear face to this sense. See how much inner turmoil you still carry from this experience: Were you hurt by [name or description of person]? How hurtful was this act or series of acts by [name or description of person]? Do you think that what you experienced with [name or description of person] has negatively affected your inner world?

Which Person Is Primary in Wounding You?

Examine your responses to all of those identified in the preceding exercise. Add up the ratings for the second and third questions. Who received the highest score? In this case, *high* does not get the person the gold star. Instead, he or she or they get the goodness of forgiveness from you in the next chapter. With courage in hand, try to rank the people from the one who has done the most damage to the one who has done, relatively speaking, the least damage. This, then, is your list for the work in the next chapter.

To aid you even further in knowing whether or not you need forgiveness for self-healing, let's go deeper now and examine the extent of your psychological injuries. The more hurt you have incurred, the more important it is to forgive, at least for the purpose of your experiencing emotional healing.

Examining Your Inner World

The purpose of this section is to help you explore, as gently as possible, seven inner wounds—or sources of inner turmoil—that you may have suffered. You were introduced to many of these in Key 1 when we explored why forgiveness matters and the psychological benefits of forgiveness. Here you will explore them in a different way, as they may or may not apply directly to you.

First, know that it is okay to have inner wounds. It does not make you a bad person or inferior to other people. We are *all* wounded at some points in our lives. If we could take a poll of all people within one mile of your residence, it is likely that over 90% of the adults would tell you that, right now, they are carrying internal wounds in need of healing. You are not alone.

The seven inner wounds that we will examine here may not be caused entirely by others' injustice. However, your being aware of the link between the injustice you experienced and any of the themes we are about to discuss might be insightful for you. As just one example, if you have anxiety and cannot pinpoint the cause, you might drift toward negative, self-directed statements such as "I'm a weak person," or "I let too much bother me," or "What's wrong with me?" If you do not make the next link between reducing the anxiety and forgiving certain people, then you may not receive the maximum amount of care for your emotional wounds. Forgiveness as a component of psychotherapy has been long overlooked and so some psychotherapists may miss this point.

When you are ready, take a look at the first of these seven inner wounds.

Anxiety

Every living person has felt anxiety at one time or another. This anxiety can range from a mild sense of internal unease to fear to dread to absolute panic. It is one of the most unpleasant emotions you can have because it disrupts your inner peace. Do you have anxiety? Or is this one of the disruptive feelings that is not an issue for you? If you do have anxiety, is it something generally present, or is it specific to a particular person, place, or undertaking/task/job? Sometimes when we have been hurt by another, even in very specific ways, we still feel the anxiety generally, in a vague and diffused way, because our trust is now damaged. The person has stolen our safe feeling, and so we live with a general feeling of fear. If you do have anxiety, is it slight, only showing up from time to time and not disrupting you? Is it more than that, more intense, but still not disrupting your life? Or is the anxiety getting in your way, disturbing your sleep or energy or concentration? Is the anxiety sabotaging your happiness? If it is disruptive to how you live your life and if it is smothering your happiness, you need to address it for the sake of your own well-being.

As you will see, we will not target the anxiety itself. Forgiveness is focused on the one who hurt you, and as you do that, with the goodness of mercy and even love, the anxiety is likely to lessen. So take a breath and relax your body because when you forgive those who are most responsible for this uncomfortable feeling, it is likely to diminish.

Depression

Depression is a kind of sadness that contributes to feeling fatigued and disinterested overall, in what for you are generally pleasurable activities. It can range from a mild sense of sadness to a deep sense of worthlessness. It is not so sharp a feeling as is anxiety. Instead, it is more like a mood, and moods linger more than feelings do. This is one of the most unpleasant moods you can have because it disrupts your inner world and, when severe, affects your everyday functioning. Do you think that you may have depression? Or is this one of the disruptive moods that is not an issue for you? If you suspect that you are depressed, it is best to consult a mental health professional for an evaluation. If you are feeling down, is it generally present, dampening your daily life, or is it more of a sadness that is associated with a particular person, place, or undertaking/task/job? Sometimes when we have been hurt by another, even in very specific ways, we still feel depressed generally, in a vague and diffused way. If this general depressed state is present for most of the day, every day, over more than two weeks, then the diagnosis of major depression is usually considered by a mental health care professional. Major depression can be addressed medically through medication. I recommend professional help not only for diagnosing major depression but also for treating it.

If you have a mood that seems depressed to you (and not just temporary feelings of sadness, which affect all people from time to time), is it slight, coming to visit from time to time and not disrupting you? Is it more than that, more intense but not disrupting your life? Or is the depressed mood getting in your way, disrupting sleep or energy or concentration? Is the depression disrupting your happiness? If it is disruptive to how you live your life and if it is smothering your happiness, you need to address this. And again, if your depression is deep and lasting two or more weeks, please seek professional help. Today's medications can be very effective in lessening the symptoms. Keep in mind that if there is a psychological cause of the depression, then medication alone will not be sufficient. You will have to get to the root cause of the depression for you to be healed. Some people think that depression is caused only by an imbalance in brain neurotransmitters and therefore cannot be cured, only medicated. I disagree with this view. As you know, there are scientific data to show that incest survivors, upon forgiving the men who violated them, not only showed reductions in depression but they actually became *non*depressed. And that improvement was still there 14 months after the forgiveness treatment had ended.

Unhealthy Anger

We discussed the general meaning of unhealthy anger in Key 1. Unhealthy anger is characterized by a heightened intensity that abides within the person. Consider a pilot light and the subsequent flame. Unhealthy anger is like living with the flame continually (or at least too often) ignited inside. It is time now to examine your pattern of anger to see if it is unhealthy. If a person lets unhealthy anger settle in and grow in intensity, it is almost like a disease in need of cure. I have never heard medical professionals refer to unhealthy anger as "a disease," but perhaps someone has and I just missed it. Once anger becomes unhealthy, it is hard to reduce it other than temporarily. As it takes hold in a person's body, it affects all aspects of his or her life.

Living for many months or even years with chronic, unhealthy anger can contribute to the development of severe anxiety and depression. If you have unhealthy anger, consider the possibility that it could contribute to further psychological complications that need professional assistance to quiet the symptoms. The professional literature has noted for some time that severe anxiety and depression are often accompanied by intense and abiding anger. In our book *Forgiveness Therapy* for psychiatrists, psychologists, and other helping professionals, Dr. Fitzgibbons and I show this connection between anger and other disruptive feelings and moods and how forgiveness can reduce the anger first and then these other troubling consequences of being treated unfairly. It is possible to reverse this "disease" of unhealthy anger with an effective antidote: forgiveness. If unhealthy anger has become a part of your very being, then forgiveness can give you your life back.

Ask the same kinds of questions about anger that you asked about anxiety and depression. If you do have anger within you, is it slight, showing up from time to time and not disrupting you? Is it more than that, more intense, but still not disrupting your life? Or is the anger getting in your way, sapping your energy, and sabotaging the quality of your relationships? Is the anger disrupting your happiness? If it is disruptive to how you live your life and if it is smothering your happiness, you need to address it for the sake of your own well-being.

Lack of Trust

Unjust treatment can be sinister if it robs you of your trust in people in general. When a partner ends a relationship, the person being left has to be on guard against conclusions such as "No man can be trusted" or "All women are just out for themselves." Depending on what kind of unjust treatment you experienced, your trust could be damaged in specific areas or it could have generalized to all people. The adolescent who is benched by the coach might conclude that all coaches are rats. At the same time, if this issue of athletics is a major part of the adolescent's life, he or she may conclude: "All people make dumb decisions and those decisions can hurt me. I have to watch my back with everyone!"

A lack of trust can have the added effect of preventing healthy relations long after that one person hurt you. You might have anxiety now in a new relationship, even if the new person is wonderful. This is because you are carrying the wound from the previous relationship into all new ones until you deal, head on, with the damaged trust.

In the paragraph above, I used the word *anxiety* in this section on lack of trust. I did so because the issues we are addressing here do not fit into little airtight boxes. Deep and long-lasting anxiety can become associated with depression, and then the depression leads to a lack of trust. The issues can be interrelated in that a person suffers from several of them at the same time.

Let's ask the usual questions now. If you do generally mistrust other people, is it slight, popping up from time to time and not disrupting you? Is it more than that, more intense, but still not disrupting your life? Or is the mistrust getting in your way, disturbing the quality of your relationships with others, particularly with persons who are very important to you? Is the mistrust blanketing your happiness? If it is disruptive to how you live your life and if it is smothering your happiness, you need to address it for the sake of your own well-being.

Forgiveness by itself is only a part of restoring trust. Forgiveness reduces the anger that might prevent you from even beginning another relationship. If you resume the relationship that has been damaged by injustice, you also will need to practice just/fair behavior, asking the person to genuinely alter the behavior that was damaging.

Low Self-Esteem and Lack of Confidence

As I began this journey of studying forgiveness, I was unaware of the following conclusion, but now I have seen it enough that I can confidently share it with you. Do you know who the one person is whom you probably dislike the most as a result of others' cruelty toward you? *Yourself.* When others hurt us, we end up not liking ourselves, even more than we dislike the one(s) who hurt us.

I hear, over and over, people saying something to the effect of, "I'm worthless. See how worthless I am? This could only happen to a worthless person!" People who have been hurt by others who held power over them and then withdrew love become, in essence, brainwashed by the implied or stated messages of their unworthiness. They then internalize the negative messages and falsely conclude: "Well, I suppose this is true. I *am* worthless." And the other, who wants to dominate, wins.

A lack of confidence is related to, but different from, a lack of trust. Trust is outward-directed, toward others; we end up with pessimism toward other people. With a lack of confidence, we end up with pessimism toward ourselves.

Surely, it is not right that you may be walking around with low self-esteem (not liking yourself so much) and low confidence (pessimism about your ability to move forward in life) because another person is wounded inside. That person's wounds should not become your own internal wounds, and the process described in this book is intended to help you move out of this lie about who you are and what you can accomplish. If you think about it, this is another form of injustice against you. The first injustice was the other's actions of unfairness toward you. This then led to the development of this new injustice of doubting yourself.

Now to our familiar questions, this time focused on self-esteem and confidence in yourself. If you do have low self-worth, is it slight, popping up from time to time but not really disrupting you? Is it more than that, more intense, but still not disrupting your life? Or is the continual inner voice of "I can't . . ." getting in your way, disrupting the quality of life? Is your low self-esteem disrupting your happiness? If low self-esteem and lack of confidence are disruptive to how you live your life and if they are smothering your happiness, you need to address both areas for the sake of your own well-being.

The Negative Worldview

We are talking here of your general philosophy of life. Who are human beings in their very essence? Are most people out for themselves, including you? Is there much love left in the world? Are you and others incapable of putting more love into the world? Why are you here on this planet?

All of these questions form your story of what this world is, how it works, and what is the essential nature of the people who inhabit our planet. People who have been treated cruelly by others tend to slide, almost unknowingly, into a kind of general pessimism so that the glass is perpetually half-empty rather than half-full. Such a doomsday perspective can lead to anxiety, depression, unhealthy anger, mistrust, and low self-esteem. In other words, think about your psychological health this way: A person gravely wounds you. You react with anger. Over time the anger deepens, giving way to discouragement or even depression, which lowers your self-image and fuels an even deeper pessimism or negative worldview. This deepened pessimism then circles back and deepens the anger . . . which deepens the depression . . . and deeper and deeper you go. We have to stop this downward spiral somewhere along its path by short-circuiting the unhealthy anger, or going after that pessimistic worldview, or by first treating the symptoms of anxiety and depression medically, so that you have the energy and clarity of mind to stop the descent into pessimism that could destroy you. Do you see that we have many places to confront unhealthy anger? It is forgiveness that can enter at any one of these places along your journey (at the unhealthy anger station or the depression station or the pessimistic worldview station) and stop that part of the journey for you and for those you love—who now will get a "new you" as a gift to them.

Reminder 25:

You can overcome the negative circumstances in your life from being treated unfairly, using forgiveness as the antidote.

Let's consider the important questions asked about the other issues in this section. If you do have a negative worldview, how negative is it? Is it mild and perhaps blended with more realistic thinking that there really are some good people out there? Or is the negative worldview getting in your way, disrupting the quality of your life? Is the negative worldview dampening your happiness? If it is disruptive to how you live your life and if it is smothering your happiness, you need to address it for the sake of your own well-being.

One More Issue: Lack of Confidence in Overcoming the Negative

As you read this, with your reduced energy and possibly some discouragement because of the mistreatment, you might be saying something like this to yourself: "When I look up from the pit I'm in, I see no way out." This, too, is the big lie intended to keep you under the power of others. Discouragement is a way to keep you from developing the confidence that you can and will change. The lack of confidence leads you to give in to the other's power over you. And you surely do not want that. Try a change of pace; stand up to the lie that you cannot get out of the pit, even if you can't *feel* confident just yet. Bet on yourself. You can and you will overcome this lack of confidence and the strength of forgiveness will help you to heal.

Exercise #2: The Test of Your Inner World

Record your answers to the following seven statements by rating each on a scale of 1–5:

1 = not at all
2 = to a small extent
3 = to a moderate extent
4 = to a large extent
5 = to an extreme extent

1. I'm anxious.
2. I'm depressed.
3. I have unhealthy anger inside of me.

4. I lack trust in other people.
5. I don't like myself.
6. My worldview is negative.
7. I don't think that I'll be able to overcome my wounded inner world.

If you gave a rating of 4 or 5 to any of these statements, then you need to work on healing your inner world through the process of forgiveness. As you can see, the higher the score, the more pervasive are your wounds. The scale ranges from a low score of 7 to a high score of 35. A high score of 5 on anxiety, depression, unhealthy anger, *and* self-esteem suggest to me that you should consider getting some professional help for the symptoms if they are long-lasting and disruptive to your everyday functioning.

Keep these scores for later; we will revisit them in Key 8.

Where Do We Start? The Practice Person

In the next chapter you can begin to forgive one person who has hurt you and left enough wounds in your heart to warrant the important work of forgiveness. From your work in this chapter, choose one person who has hurt you, but not at the deepest level. Beginning with the one person who has hurt you the deepest may be too much to start. At the same time, this needs to be a meaningful exercise for you, so review the people you listed in Exercise #1 of this chapter and choose one who is near the top of the list in terms of your amount of emotional pain when you think about him or her. Remember that if you are feeling overwhelmed at any point as you do the exercises in Key 4, then put the book down for now and take a break. Talk with a friend, relax, find time to refresh. If you are unable to continue by yourself, remember that I and others are taking questions at www.internationalforgiveness.com. If your reaction is such that you think you need to talk with a counselor or therapist about your inner wounds from this person or other people, I urge you to do so. Sometimes inner wounds need professional care, and I encourage you to recognize this and seek the appropriate help. There is no dishonor, only courage, knowing you need assistance.

Who, then, is this practice person? Name him or her and go through Keys 4 and 5 with this one person in mind. Select others from your list in Key 3 until you are ready for the one person who has wounded you the most. For the one who is the most challenging to forgive, I recommend that you first go through Key 6, "When It's Hard to Forgive," and then try to forgive him or her by coming back to Keys 4–5 and then 8. All of the prior work should help you to forgive him or her.

As one final note, in Key 4 we will not address the seven consequences of injustice—the sources of inner turmoil—discussed here. In forgiveness therapy, for example, the therapist does not focus on the symptoms of emotional disruption (unless immediate attention is required, such as the need for medication). Instead, the therapist asks the person to reach beyond him- or herself to the other, to the one who was unjust. In this merciful reaching out, based on our scientific studies, you will begin to experience emotional healing. We will come back to the seven consequences of injustice and the sources of inner turmoil in Key 8.

Now let's begin to develop the mind of forgiveness.

KEY 4

DEVELOP THE MIND
OF FORGIVENESS

The world is such a hurting place. Civil society asks each person to walk within the community as if he or she were not wounded. Yet the forgiving mind asks this of us: See beyond the current fashion, beyond the forced smile, to the other's heart, which likely is bleeding today.

It's time to become forgivingly fit by exercising your brain. Now that you've identified the source of your pain and inner turmoil, the next step is to prepare your mind to forgive. This is where you use the fourth key to open the door to the *mind of forgiveness*. This, however, is not a gym; this is the area where you live your life. You will be training your mind to think in a new way about a person who hurt you. You will be examining some of the details of that person's life so that you can see more clearly what wounds he or she carries. This change in mindset can go a long way in learning how to forgive.

As you train your mind to forgive, you might be interested to know that a group of neuroscientists in Italy has actually begun to map the area of the brain that develops as you do this kind of forgiveness thinking. Dr. Emiliano Ricciardi and his colleagues at the University of Pisa published a study in the journal *Frontiers in Human Neuroscience* in 2013. They discovered that when people successfully imagined forgiving someone in a hypothetical story (one that was made up for the experiment and not actually experienced by the participants), then those participants showed increased activity in "the precuneus, right inferior parietal regions, and the dorsolateral prefrontal cortex" of the brain.[9] This is the same brain network that is activated in other studies when a person is showing empathy to others. Before giving this area of your brain a good workout, let's start with a case study.

Warm-Up to Encountering the One Who Hurt You: A Case Study

Harold grew up in a two-parent family with his sister, Nadine. Their father was a public defender who worked long, hard hours defending people who could not afford legal counsel. The father's clients often did not appreciate his efforts and tended to blame him if court decisions did not go their way, leaving him repeatedly discouraged and resentful.

Harold's mother herself had a very domineering mother who was highly anxious and controlling. In a psychological sense Harold's mother inherited this pattern of anxiety, but without the feature of trying to tightly control everything as a way to minimize the anxiety. Harold, in turn, "inherited" *his* mother's anxiety.

Harold, with this anxiety within him as a child, struggled academically in school. He was quiet and shy and thus a target for those who bully. In childhood, Harold began to suffer from low self-esteem. In adolescence and early adulthood, he was too shy to begin dating and so in his adult years he had to learn those skills that others had acquired earlier. This delayed development added to his sense of low self-worth. His struggles with anxiety were beginning to make him angry, yet he never drew the connection between his anxiety, his father's disenchantment at work, and his mother's own considerable anxiety.

---

[9] Ricciardi, E., Rota, G., Sani, L., Gentili, C., Gaglianese, A., Guazzelli, M., & Petrini, P. (2013). How the brain heals emotional wounds: the functional neuroanatomy of forgiveness. *Frontiers in Human Neuroscience, 7*, article 839, 1–9 (quotation is from page 1). doi: 10.3389/fnhum.2013.00839

After a series of failed relationships with women, Harold's resentment peaked. He started to use dating as a way of fulfilling his own physical needs and so he began to disrespect women, not unlike the way students had disrespected him in school in earlier years. Eventually, he did find a woman, Patricia, to marry, with whom he had a son, Ethan. The marriage, however, did not work out. Harold continued to show much self-centered behavior, culminating in an affair. The marriage degenerated, ending in divorce. Ethan was nine years old at the time of the divorce.

When Ethan reached adulthood, he, too, showed signs of generalized anxiety and he sought a psychotherapist's help in overcoming it. He presented with much anger directed at his father for leaving the family. Ethan saw his father's flaws and when the psychotherapist suggested that they probe more deeply into the father's personality, doing so only intensified Ethan's anger. He was looking for support for his anger and confirmation that his father was an unfair man.

The therapist then had an unexpected idea: that Ethan should begin to see his father from a wider-angle lens. Ethan sat down with his aunt Nadine and began to see his father from a different perspective—and he was surprised by what he saw. He came to realize that Harold was hurt by both his father's bitterness at his work and his mother's considerable anxiety. He understood the childhood struggles and his father's self-doubts. He saw the pattern—a weakness in this particular emotion of anxiety—that seemed to travel across the generations. He, too, had a similar pattern toward both his grandmother and father. When Ethan saw all of his father's struggles, he was more motivated to forgive him for the divorce and the consequence of his growing up without his father. He did not see an evil man now. Yes, he saw a man who made some very bad choices, but these bad choices did not reduce Harold to someone who is less than human. His father, though wounded and confused, was and is a person, just like Ethan is. These insights helped Ethan to reduce resentment, become psychologically healthy, and move on with his life. Coupled with forgiveness, these deep insights helped to heal him emotionally.

Preliminary Steps to Developing a Forgiving Mind

For the exercises in this chapter, it is important that you have completed the work in Key 2 so that you are in the process of becoming forgivingly fit. If you are not confident yet that this transformation is taking place, spend more time with Key 2 and do the exercises there until your feel more comfortable with this way of looking at the world.

Bring to mind the person you selected in the previous chapter. The first step in this part of the process is to get to know the person who has hurt you by going through a series of exercises that focus on his or her childhood and move slowly through his or her life-span so that you get an increasingly expanded view of the person with the help of a series of questions for you to consider. You will likely not know the exact answer to all these questions. Just do the best you can with the information you have.

At times in the exercises, you will be asked to think back into the person's distant past to see this person as a young child. The point is not to make up what happened then, but instead to use your knowledge of what it means to be a person as you think about the one who hurt you. At other times, you will be asked to project into the future and imagine a likely scenario for the one who hurt you. Again, this step is not about fabricating a story. It's about thinking of some probable results that could occur—that would be likely—if he or she were to continue on the current path, given the patterns you have seen and experienced firsthand.

Exercise #1: Visualizing the Person as an Infant

Imagine that the person who hurt you is a newborn. This is an innocent child with a lot of challenges ahead. He cannot even roll over by himself. (Note: If the person who hurt you is/was female, mentally substitute feminine pronouns throughout this step.) He cannot feed himself or take care of any of his needs whatsoever.

What kind of a home or situation is this person born into? Is there love in this family? How do you know—what is your evidence? Does this helpless infant deserve anything less than lots of love and care? What if he does not get enough attention? How will that lack affect his attachment to his mother? Research studies have shown for decades that if an infant does not receive attention and love from the primary caregiver, then the all-important issue of attachment will be damaged. Attachment for an infant is a healthy and necessary part of becoming a full, healthy person in a psychological sense. If the attachment is weak because the caretaker cannot attend well to the infant's needs, then trust as an adult likely will be damaged, and, as we have seen, a lack of trust is painful. It prevents the person from getting close to others. A lack of attachment can set a trajectory of loneliness and conflict for this little baby when he reaches maturity.

What do you know of his attachment as an infant? Is there anyone you can ask about this to gain insight? Has the person himself given you any indication of how he was raised? Did his mother and father have time for him, play with him, nurture him, and do so with a willing heart? If not, then this innocent infant has experienced a kind of psychological trauma from the time of birth. This is not to say that you should now excuse the injustices you have suffered from this person. However, it *is* to say that this is now part of this person's story and that you should make note of it.

Exercise #2: Visualizing the Inherent Worth of This Infant

Visualize the one who hurt you as she is an infant. (Note: If the person who hurt you is/was male, mentally substitute masculine pronouns throughout this step.) Look at her in her crib, lying there with all of the potential in the world. She asks for very little, only to be loved and to have her basic needs met. At this point, she has never hurt anyone in her short life. Because she now shares a common humanity with all people in this world, we can say that she possesses inherent worth. By this I mean that her worth is built in and need not be earned. She does not have to be the perfect child to have inherent worth. She does not have to be perfect physically to have inherent worth. Her sleeping and eating habits have nothing at all to do with her being special, unique, and irreplaceable. Inherent worth includes these attributes: to be special, unique, and irreplaceable.

Again visualize this infant in the crib. Look down upon her and say, "This little baby has inherent worth."

Exercise #3: Visualizing the Person as a Child

What do you know of his childhood? (Note: If the person who hurt you is/was female, mentally substitute feminine pronouns throughout this step.) Try to ask others—or even him, if it is appropriate to do so. A central question is this: What wounds did he incur from others when he was a child? Make note of those wounds and see them in the context of the previous visualization—the one in which we saw an innocent infant in the crib. This person has not deserved these wounds.

Now see this child taking his very first steps. See the hesitancy, the fear, and also the courage to take those steps. Learning to walk is a universal triumph of the human spirit and the one who hurt you is showing that spirit of courage and the need to grow.

See now his first disappointment with other children, perhaps his own brother or sister. In that sibling's frustrations, that other child might have been selfish, impatient, even physically abusive. Yes, children are quickly over these kinds of things, but the wounds can be held deep in the heart if the hurt happens frequently. Do you have any evidence of this child being treated in an insensitive way by other children who perhaps wanted to dominate?

What do you know of how his mother and father treated

him as a child? Was there any subtle neglect or criticism that went into his heart, wounding him in such a way that the wound remained into adulthood, only to be passed to you? Are you aware of any patterns in which a parent was harsh? Did the child have to endure any kind of abandonment? If so, this can be one of the cruelest cuts of all to the human heart. It is very unfair and can be a source of pain for decades.

What of school experiences? Do you think that he was ever bullied? Bullying can leave an enduring wound. Bullying—which is a series of ongoing behaviors intended to demean—can damage the victim's self-esteem. Was he demeaned? Think about this: The innocent infant, who never wounded anyone, is now being treated on the school grounds as if he has no inherent worth. This is not to condone this person's actions against you. They were wrong and they remain wrong. The point is to help you to expand your view of who this person is.

Exercise #4: Visualizing the Person as an Adolescent

For this exercise, try to gather information on what adolescence was like for her. (Note: If the person who hurt you is/ was male, mentally substitute masculine pronouns throughout this step.) A key feature of adolescence is to establish one's identity, who one is as a person, what one values and why. So a key issue here is this: Did anyone hurt this young person to such an extent that her identity became confused? If so, how was her identity confused? Did she begin to develop self-doubts and to what extent?

Another important characteristic of adolescence is the forging of strong relationships with peers and to begin entering the world of dating. Were there any difficulties with peers that could have wounded her? If so, try to be specific here. What story might she have begun to tell herself about her own worthiness?

For some who tended to get their way a lot in the high school years, there is a possibility of developing narcissism, or an exaggerated sense of one's own self-importance. We are all important because we all have inherent worth. Yet sometimes people begin to think that *they* are more special and unique than others. It is here that narcissism can creep into a person's personality. When that happens, the person might come to believe that her needs are more important than yours, and the result can be misery for both of you.

Some adolescents go in the opposite direction of narcissism because of the emotional wounds they have received and conclude that they are less worthy than everyone else. The low self-esteem can lead some adolescents into excessive anger as they express their frustrations. You might have been a victim of this low self-esteem and the resultant anger in the one who hurt you.

What, then, were this person's formative adolescent years like in terms of the emotional wounds she received?

Exercise #5: Visualizing the Person as a Young Adult

A key to young adulthood is to begin to forge a meaningful partnership with another. As you can imagine, if a person brings wounds from infancy, childhood, and adolescence into this new partnership, there is a high probability of conflict. Part of the conflict is that the unsuspecting partner now will inherit, in a psychological sense, those wounds. In fact, both people may end up wounding each other because of their past history.

Many people with whom I speak are unaware of this. They do not realize that past harms are often brought into a new partnering relationship, and now the two not only have to adjust to one another but also to the ones who live in the other's heart because of resentments carried to the present time.

You may not have been the one who was, or is, the partner of the person we are thinking about. Either way, think
about how he (or she) successfully or unsuccessfully navi-
gated this important early adult step of partnering. What
wounds were inflicted on him by the partner? What wounds
did he inflict, possibly receiving even more wounds back
because of his wounding the other?

Can you see how the accumulation of wounds in this
person has weighted him down? Can you see a vulnerable
person as you think of him? Can you see a confused person? Maybe you are also seeing a scared person. Wounds
can do that—scare the person—and then he feels as if he
has to defend his turf. This can lead to anger and harsh
words by him and by you, if you were the recipient of those
words. Again, this is not to disavow the injustice you experienced. It really was and is an injustice. At the same time,
it's important that you begin to exercise that area of your
brain that activates empathy for the one who hurt you, as a
person, as someone in need of healing.

Exercise #6: Visualizing the Person in Middle Adulthood

A key feature to middle adulthood is to make a contribution in the world of work and to provide for the next generation, either by raising one's own children or providing
help to others' children through service work and even
teaching.

When you see a person who is just stuck and cannot
contribute to others' welfare at this stage of life, sometimes
it is because the person is so distracted by her (or his) own
inner wounds that she does not have the energy and the
focus to get the job done. When you are struggling, for
example, with a virus, it is hard to concentrate on anything
else. It can be similar with emotional wounds. Think of
them as a kind of virus that weighs a person down.

Might this have happened to the one who hurt you? At

this point you might be saying, "But the one who hurt me is not yet in middle adulthood." If this is the case, then imagine what middle adulthood might be like once she reaches this stage of life and is still very wounded inside. Think of how she might take a pattern of interacting with others now into the middle adult years. What would she be like as a person then?

Can you see the struggles waiting for her? Can you see the possibility of an emotional spiral downward if she does not get help with those wounds? If so, you have just given the empathy center of your brain a good workout. Now the question is this: What can you do in a concrete way for the one who hurt you? How can you aid her so that she meets middle adulthood in a much better way than the scenario you just created? Do you realize that you have an opportunity to help this person navigate the important stages of adult life if she allows you near her and if she is not a danger to you?

Exercise #7: Visualizing the Person in Later Years

The psychologist Erik Erikson, in observing how people change over time, stated in his book, *Childhood and Society*, that one of the most important developments in the elderly years is to have what he called *integrity*. Integrity basically means the state of being whole, in this case, in a psychological sense. In the elderly years, integrity is in tension with what he calls despair, or living with regrets that are now difficult to change. Note that integrity includes having few regrets.

The one who hurt you may not be elderly yet and so you may have to do another imaginary exercise here, but that is all right. Try to see the person who hurt you as he is approaching the end of life. What will that life be like if he does not seek forgiveness? Try to step inside his shoes for a moment and imagine the inner pain of a life in which he let his wounds rule him and be imposed on other people, including you. Can you get a sense of the burden he is carrying? Try to see the inner torment that is a part of him and recognize how he can do little now to reverse the pain that he has caused you and perhaps many others. Can you feel his sadness, his bitterness? Spend a little time imagining him at this point in his life and see if you soften, even a little, toward him.

What can you do, when you are ready, to help make his elderly years less miserable for him? Can you show him that he has inherent worth? Do you think he even realizes that he has inherent worth? If he cannot see that, can you be his teacher now? It would be an amazing gift to give.

Reminder 26:

The way a person lives his or her life now will have consequences for his or her well-being much later in life. A person who wounds others now may feel the effects of this in his or her elderly years.

Questions about Visualizing the Person across the Lifespan

Now that you have taken a sweeping perspective of the life of the person you are going to forgive first, consider these two questions that some clients ask once they start the forgiveness process.

Question 1

"Having tried these new perspectives, I cannot help but feel that I'm finding excuses for the person's hurtful acts. How is it that I am *not* making excuses? Sometimes I feel guilty being angry at someone who was hurt so much."

The central issue here is the person's free will regarding what he or she decides to do with all of those wounds. There is no psychological theory or finding anywhere to show that as a person is emotionally wounded, then he or she must, without exception, do certain, particular things such as insult or hit you or another. We all have a wide range of choices in how we deal with our own wounds. We have to remember that this person chose to act in these particular ways when other options were open. Therefore, he or she has to own the fact that wrongdoing was done. He or she *did* act unfairly.

Question 2

This question gets a bit philosophical in its answer, so feel free to skip it if the idea of "materialism" does not apply to you. If, however, it does apply to you, then you may be challenged by the ideas. Here is the statement and the question:

> "I do not think there is such a thing as free will because recent studies show that chemical imbalances in the brain can make certain actions more likely than others. Do you agree? For example, if a person is low in serotonin, this chemical imbalance can induce depressive symptoms that make the person's typical behavior lethargic and typical feelings turn to sadness or even hopelessness. How can that leave any room for free will?"

The two examples of behavior and feelings surrounding depression are not moral actions that directly impact upon the rights of others. Being lethargic or feeling sad or even hopeless do not in any way suggest that the person has to act in ways that are disrespectful to others. Yes, we might better understand hurtful behaviors if they occur in a person with depression, but we do not then toss out the theme of justice and pretend that the person is somehow exonerated from being just because of the low serotonin.

If it is assumed that all behavior can be explained only by material causes such as brain neurotransmitters, then we must realize the consequences of this assumption. The central consequence would be the invalidation of any moral concepts such as "right and wrong," "justice," and "forgiveness" because these concepts suggest that there is a person making his or her own decisions on matters involving other people. How can one even consider forgiving someone "who just could not help it" because of a particular brain function? The short answer is that we cannot even consider forgiving in such a scenario because to forgive is to say to oneself, in one form or another: "He did wrong, and in that wrong he hurt me. I will now try to show love for this person who acted badly." Taking this materialistic view of how the person operates leads invariably to two conclusions: (1) She did not engage in a moral (intentional, goal-directed, freely willed) act at all (because she does not have a free will to do this); and (2) the person she hurt cannot love her, in the sense of serving her for her own good, because love itself is a moral virtue that would not exist in this materialist perspective. Materialist approaches to how the world works would say that the hurt person has not freely chosen to love because brain mechanisms are responsible. Thus, moral language would make no sense.

Seeing the Person as Being Influenced by Power

The exercise in this section examines how the perspective of power (again, in its negative sense of power *over* others) may have influenced, and is currently influencing, the one who hurt you. First, a review of those two opposing views of the world: power and love.

Here are 10 pairs of contrasting statements differentiating between power and love, which may be useful in helping you forgive:

Power says, "Me first."
Love asks, "How may I serve you today?"

Power manipulates.
Love builds up.

Power exhausts others.
Love refreshes them.

Power is rarely happy in any true sense.
Love understands happiness.

Power is highly rewarded in cultures that worship money.
Love considers money to be a means to an end, not an end itself.

Power steps on others.
Love is a bridge to others' betterment.

Power wounds—even the one who exerts the power.
Love binds up the wounds, even in the self.

Power is joyless even when it is in control.
Love includes joy.

Power does not understand love.
Love does understand power and is not impressed.

Power see forgiveness as weakness and so, in rejecting forgiveness, resentments might remain.
Love sees forgiveness as a strength and so works to eliminate resentment.

Power rarely lasts because it eventually turns inward, exhausting itself. Look at slavery in the United States, or the supposedly all-powerful "Thousand-Year Reich" of the Nazis, or even the presence of the Berlin Wall, intended to imprison thought, freedom, and persons . . . forever. Love endures even in the face of grave power against it.

Exercise #8: Seeing More Clearly the Person at the Time of the Injury

You now are about to use your clearer vision to put together what I call "the power story" of the one who hurt you. By this I mean that you will have an opportunity to see how this person's ways of interacting in the world might have been shaped by the cruelty of power *against* him or her. You can use the 10 pairs of contrasting statements (listed above) to help you craft this story of the other person at the time of the offense that you currently are considering.

Let's use Key 2 even more specifically than in Key 2 to further develop your mind of forgiveness. Focus on the issues pressing in on the one who hurt you at the particular time that she (or he) hurt you deeply. Even if she had an ongoing pattern of injury toward you, try to choose one time that cut particularly deeply into your heart. Now let's see how power *against her* might have weakened her at this time when you were hurt.

- *First consideration.* At the time of the injury, was someone exerting a "me first" power play over your injurer? If so, how do you think this affected your injurer inside? This question is not about excusing the behavior of the person who injured you, but rather so that you can better understand your injurer's heart.
- *Second consideration.* Are you aware of anyone manipulating your injurer at the time that she exerted power over you? Alice was in a small company in which five people were laid off from work within a one-month period. Her employer threatened Alice with being released from her position if she did not immediately take on more responsibility at work. She increased her weekly hours, became tired, and then became deeply angry, taking out her frustrations on her best friend, who had no clue about

why she was suddenly being treated with disrespect. The friend became the recipient of Alice's misdirected anger as a result of Alice's being the victim of her boss's power play. The manipulation of her work hours proved to be too much for her in the short run.

Can you see anything like this for your injurer? Was he or she a victim of another's unjust manipulation? Add this piece to your story of who your injurer is.

• *Third consideration.* Was your injurer exhausted for some reason at the time of the offense against you? If so, what or who was exhausting him? Do not condone what happened to you. Exhaustion is not an excuse to be unkind. At the same time, are you seeing a vulnerable person in front of you?

• *Fourth consideration.* What was making your injurer unhappy at the time of this incident? Was it something inside of her? Might it even have been the wounds from her own childhood that came roaring out? Do you see the power of unhappiness? It can spread, making others unhappy, including you. Who is this unhappy person who hurt you?

• *Fifth consideration.* What part did money play in the injury? Was the person overworking for it or under pressure for it or blaming you for some financial issue? Here the point is to see a person whose priorities were not clear. He might have prioritized money over you. Money is a thing— you are a person. Add this piece to your story: Your injurer was not seeing with clearer vision and so hurt you while caught by a short-sighted worldview.

• *Sixth consideration.* When we are stepped on, it hurts. Think of the other's heart and what her injury of you must have felt like inside of her to inflict that kind of pain on another human being.

• *Seventh consideration.* Can you see the inner turmoil or even chaos inside him? He is wounded, perhaps terribly wounded.

- *Eighth consideration.* What of the joy inside her? Was there any joy at all in her at the time of your injury? What does this tell you about her? What is your clearer vision helping you to see?
- *Ninth consideration.* Because power does not understand love, the one who hurt you likely did not see your inner wounds, which need support, nurturance, and love. He did not see the inner hurt you already carried and added another wound to your heart. He passed more pain into the world by putting it into your heart. Who are you seeing? Continue creating the story.
- *Tenth consideration.* Some day the one who injured you will die. The power will end. We now have to make sure that the *consequences* of that power do not continue in this world and, like a virus, jump from you to one more person. Can you see that? The power that comes from the resulting resentment and disruption can stop now. The one who injured you had that opportunity to stop the pain from being passed along, but she did not take advantage of this opportunity. How are you seeing her in light of this lost opportunity? How are you seeing this opportunity now for yourself?

Reminder 27:

At the time of the injury, the person who hurt you probably was carrying significant wounds. They are now yours. What will you do with them?

Questions Concerning Exercise #8

Question 3

"I have done the exercise that you suggested and I see the stresses that the person was under. Still, this does little for my anger. Yes,

I see a wounded and even a weak person, but I still want to punch him for what he did to me. What can you suggest that I do so that I am not living with this resentment?"

Doing the exercises is not an automatic way out of resentment. It will take time for the resentment to end. I recommend this homework: At least twice a day for the next two weeks, go over the tasks in this exercise, trying to see the person more clearly at the time of the injury. Say to yourself, "I forgive [name] for hurting me at that time when he [she] was under stress. I will try to be merciful even though I did not receive either justice or mercy."

Question 4

"It is hard to see my injurer's wounds when she wounded me a hundred times more than what she is carrying around. When I try to look at her wounds, it makes me frustrated and sad because of all the wasted time and all the hurt created. Will I ever be able to overcome this?"

Yes, you will overcome this with a determined will. Sometimes we have to struggle for our healing and endure with great patience, without giving up. Do not expect too much too soon. The forgiveness journey is just that: a *journey* and a challenging one at times. Yet with practice your anger lessens a little more . . . and then a little more—until you can see the progress. As much as you are able, keep reaching out to the other person. Your mercy, extended to others, will come back to you.

Question 5

"My husband abandoned me four years ago—just got up and left because he said he needed his 'freedom.' He has a challenging alcohol problem and at the time we were together, he was in utter denial about this, refusing help. He never really was in the marriage from the beginning, basically coming and going as he pleased, staying away for days at a time. He is not coming back. I know this, my friends know this, and my counselor knows this.

Yet, when I read through the 10 questions about him 'at the time of the injury,' I find myself softening to such an extent that I want him back. And I feel guilty not pursuing reconciliation. What should I do?"

It is important that you stay strong in both mind and heart. Your softening toward him is compassion or willingness to "suffer along with" the person. It is essential to distinguish between having compassion for your husband and actually reconciling with him in the role as your husband. He was not committed to your marriage from the beginning, he abandoned you, and he has a potentially serious problem with alcohol. He does not seem capable of assuming the role of husband, not just to you but in general. He seems to be unwilling to get help for his deep problems, at least that was your reasoned impression before he left. Unless he gets that help and changes to a substantial degree, then making this distinction is likely to serve you better: "I can respect him as a person, but I cannot be a wife to him because he is incapable of being a true husband for me."

With regard to your feelings of guilt, realize, with your mind of forgiveness, that you did not initiate the abandonment. He did. You did nothing wrong. Sure, you likely were imperfect in the relationship, but all people are imperfect in all relationships. Imperfection is not a justifiable cause of four years of abandonment. Your mind of forgiveness needs to see this and believe it deeply within you. You have endured much and now it is time to see yourself as you are: a person worthy of respect, who has respected her husband under dire circumstances, and continues to have a soft heart and a mind of forgiveness toward him.

Exercise #9: Using the Global Perspective to View the Person

Even if you do not know a lot about the details of the person's life, you will be able to reflect on the questions in this exercise because it does not ask for any details. Instead, it asks what you and this person hold in common:

- *Do you need nourishment and shelter to live?* So, too, does the one who hurt you.
- *Do you need clean air to breathe and to stay healthy?* So, too, does the one who hurt you.
- *How does your inner circulatory system work? Do you have a heart and veins and arteries within?* So, too, does this person. He has the same kind of circulatory system as you.
- *Do you need the help of others to maintain a healthy body? That is, do you sometimes need medical care?* So, too, does the one who hurt you. When she has a cut on her arm, she bleeds. If her appendix should burst, she would need immediate medical attention. Her bones are vulnerable, just like yours; they can break and need repair.
- *Do you have a mind that allows you to think through important issues? Is your brain structure the same as that of a zebra, elephant, or monkey, or is it different?* The one who hurt you has the capacity to think rationally, just as you do. Your brains share much more in common than does his brain with a zebra.
- *Do you sometimes get thirsty or tired?* So, too, does the one who hurt you.
- *Have you suffered in this world?* So, too, has the one who hurt you.
- *Is your body subject to the laws of nature, in that, as you advance in age, you at first gain physical strength and then undergo a slow decline in that strength?* The one who hurt you is subject to these same laws of nature.
- *Will you die some day?* The one who hurt you is equally as vulnerable. She will die some day, too.

Look at your answers to all of these questions. Do you realize that the two of you have more in common with each other than you have differences that apparently divide you? What is it that the two of you share most in common? You share personhood. You share this: You are both special, unique, and irreplaceable.

Reminder 28:

You share a common personhood with the one who hurt you.

Exercise #10: Using the Eternal Perspective to View the Person

In 1938, the American playwright Thornton Wilder wrote what some consider to be the classic play of the 20th century: *Our Town*. The point of the play is to show the vastness of life through frequent references to *thousands of miles* or *millions of years*. Yet, despite this vastness, human meaning is found in the humble, seemingly unimportant and quickly forgotten interactions with those who, for the short moment, are alive at the exact same time as you are.

There are three acts to the play. In Act I we are introduced to a depiction of seemingly trivial interactions among people in a small, humble town, Grovers Corners, New Hampshire. Act II consists of a wedding in which we see how unconditional love is put to the test as a young man and woman join together, and in so doing, have to separate from the parents with whom they have a strong and loving connection. In Act III, we see further separations, occurring all too soon, because of death. And death in this play leads to a uniting of those who have died. Some of those who have died begin to see that those seemingly trivial interactions in Act I are precious and need to be seen, acknowledged, and lived to the full by those who are still passing through time and will quickly die.

When all three acts are viewed together, a profound theme emerges: Even though life is short and we all die, in that dying we share something of the eternal with this other person, something that will not end.

Mr. Wilder captures the eternal nature of our common

humanity with all of its suffering and striving to love in very few, but very vivid, sentences.

In one scene he lets us see the great pain in the separation of persons at death when the Stage Manager (the one with a vast vision of time and humanity) says this: "People just wild with grief have brought their relatives up to the hill. We all know how it is . . . and we're coming up here ourselves when our fit's over" (p. 81). We all share the separation from others at death and we will all share death itself.

Yet, in this play, death is not the final answer. There is more to this vast nature of humanity. Again the Stage Manager instructs us this way: "Everybody knows in their bones that something is eternal, and that something has to do with human beings. All the greatest people ever lived have been telling us that for five thousand years. . . . There's something way down deep that's eternal about every human being" (p. 81).

Every human being . . . do you share something eternal with the one who hurt you? We know that you share a short time on this earth, you share suffering while here, and you both will share dying. You have a great deal in common just by being on this earth at the same time. And yet, might you share something that never ends? As the Stage Manager says, this idea has been strong in deep thinkers for thousands of years. If you share something of the eternal with this person, what does this tell you about her? About him? Let this perspective help strengthen your mind toward forgiveness.

What, then, is the consequence of taking the eternal perspective? The Stage Manager gives us the punch line regarding forgiveness and power seeking: "enemy 'n enemy . . . money 'n miser . . . all those terribly important things kind of grow pale around here" (in the cemetery *after* death, p. 82). As you place eternity next to the injustice that happened to you, the point is not to diminish what you experienced. What happened to you was wrong.

At the same time, how significant will it be in 10 billion years plus 10 billion years and beyond that? Will this person still be, as the Stage Manager puts it, the "enemy"?

Exercise #11: Who, Then, Is This Person?

It is time to put the entire narrative into a complete whole. Tell the story of the one who hurt you from beginning to end, first from the perspective of physical frailties, psychological suffering, and a common humanity that you share together. This is a vulnerable person, not superman or superwoman.

Now to the theme of woundedness. When did those wounds begin for the one who hurt you? When did he receive his first wound from another—a wound that cut deeply and left a mark to such a degree that he wounded you? Now complete the narrative of the wounds. Which wounds occurred for him in later childhood, adolescence, and beyond, shaping who this person is? And what will he become if he does not confront those wounds? Now focus on the power that was imposed upon him by others. He already was carrying wounds when you were hurt. How wounded is this person who hurt you?

Now focus on her inherent worth. Despite all that has happened to her and despite all that she has handed out to others in terms of wounds, she has built-in value that cannot be taken away, even by your disappointments, angers, and resentments, even by her own actions. She remains a person. You can see this when you take the global and eternal perspectives. This is someone who is special, unique, and irreplaceable, despite all of the wounds that she has inflicted on you and others. She is someone who transcends those wounds. You may have to struggle within yourself to develop this perspective, but it is worth that effort to develop the mind of forgiveness.

Who is the person who hurt you when you look at him, at her, in this way? Who is it that wounded you?

> **Reminder 29:**
>
> The person who hurt you is more than those wounds imposed on you.

Exercise #12: Seeing More Clearly Who You Are as a Person

It now is time to exercise your mind in relation to how you see yourself. When others hurt us, the injury tends to distort our thinking about who we are, leading us to form a negative perspective. It is time now to tell your own story to yourself. Who are you now that you are beginning to see the other person with the mind of forgiveness? Look how far you have come. Some of you, before opening this book, may have placed this person just a little lower than human. Power does that. It pushes people down. What about your vision now? Have you brought the person up to human status, deserving of basic human rights? Look to see if you have shed the power worldview in favor of the love worldview. You are seeing a full human being despite her having wounded you. You can see her unhappiness, lack of joy, confusion . . . and pain. Your eyes can now see pain in those who inflict pain on you.

> **Reminder 30:**
>
> You grow stronger as you see the one who hurt you as a wounded person, as someone who needs healing for those wounds.

Keep your clearer vision on *yourself* for a while. Do you see how far you have come—and you are only on our fourth key? You are growing as a person, expanding your vision to a considerable degree. The expanded vision is likely making you more whole inside.

Questions Concerning Exercise #12

Question 6

"Is this exercise asking me to change my entire identity—to change who I am at the core of my being? I feel kind of glued to the belief that I'm not a good person."

Yes, this exercise asks you to change your identity—which takes time and effort. You have to begin realizing that your image of yourself as "not a good person" is the big lie and you have to fight against that lie. You are sincerely struggling to change your view of someone (or more than one) who hurt you deeply. This takes much courage, patience, and love even if you do not yet see these qualities emerging in you. Keep working toward a true understanding of yourself. It is worth the effort.

Question 7

"I can get this clearer vision of myself you are talking about, but I have no love in my heart for the person who hurt me. In fact, I kind of feel repulsed when I think of him. Can I forgive without this feeling of love in my heart?"

The short answer is yes, you can forgive without feeling love in your heart for the person. However, try to see this from another angle. You might not have heard of the term *classical conditioning*. This is a psychological concept in which two things become associated by virtue of their proximity. As a child you learned to associate the sight of a flame burning on the stove with getting burned when put your hand too near it. You learned to associate the sight of that open flame on the stove with pain. So even after your little hand healed, whenever you saw the flame on the stove, at least for a while, you got nervous because you were anticipating more pain.

It is the same with a person who has hurt you: Whenever you think about or see or talk with this person, you associate him with the pain. Feeling anxious about this pain blocks any thought or feeling of love or even concern for his well-being. Changing this kind of learned response takes time, sometimes lots of time. It is possible to learn to associate your own compassion with this person. It just takes time to break the association of person–*pain* and replace it with person–*compassion*.

Exercise #13: Growing Stronger as a Person by Continuing to Explore Who You Are

Let's try a little experiment in which you go back to the first time you opened this book and read Key 1: "Know Why Forgiveness Matters and What It Is." What were your feelings then? Did you have confidence or apprehension? Did you feel energized or tired? Are you seeing yourself differently now than when you opened the book? Do you feel any stronger, more positive, more confident? If the answer is yes, then you are gaining forgiving fitness by developing the mind of forgiveness. If you are still feeling weak, try to see beyond today. The more work you do on forgiveness, the stronger you are likely to feel. Be gentle with yourself on all of this. We all grow a little at a time.

Reminder 31:

You are growing in your efforts to become forgivingly fit. You just have to keep at it to maintain the fitness.

What to Expect as You Continue to Strengthen Your Thinking about Forgiveness

First of all, congratulations on your courage to engage in what I have called the mind of forgiveness regarding someone who has caused you great pain. It is a hard but rewarding journey.

This journey, as we discussed in Key 1, is not a straight path to the end with joy quickly awaiting you. Instead, if you are like the rest of us, you will start and stop and start again a number of times before you arrive, safe, at the journey's end. You will be making great progress and then perhaps have a dream about the person and wake up angry all over again. You might think you have conquered your rage, only to encounter, unexpectedly, the person who hurt you, and there is the anger. Or perhaps it is the holiday season and you are reflecting back on your life, hoping for peace, and instead get hit by another bit of meanness from the person, and once again you are angry. The forgiveness path is quite a curving one, so be gentle with yourself. Just start again with this person by examining the nature of your wounds now, assess what kind of work you need to do (Do I need to examine her wounds? His inherent worth? Take the global and eternal perspectives?) and continue.

At other times, you will feel stalled and need a break. Any fitness program requires ample rest periods. Do not drive at the healing. Let it come to you as you do the work with moderation and wisdom.

Exercise #14: Final Thinking Exercises

Before leaving this key for now, try these last two exercises to continue strengthening your thinking, particularly about yourself. The first concerns resisting unhealthy negative statements about yourself—it is all too easy to slip into false beliefs about yourself because you are wounded. The second involves positive affirmations about you and the one who hurt you.

Every day, resist:
- The big lie that you think you are worthless because someone has treated, or even still treats, you badly.
- The lure to think that you are better off if you use power to dominate the one who dominated you.
- Another big lie of thinking that you are so broken that you cannot love.

Every day, affirm:
"I am of great worth as a person, and I do not have to earn this."

> "The one who hurt me is of great worth, not because of what [name] did, but in spite of it. This person does not have to earn this worth."
>
> "I am someone who loves. My ability to love can never be taken away from me."

In the next chapter we take up another key to your healing: finding meaning as you suffer with the wound imposed on you by another. Finding meaning in this suffering will aid your healing.

FIND MEANING IN WHAT YOU HAVE SUFFERED

I am a better person
in seeing others' pain
in being stronger
in being more loving
because I have suffered.

W hen we suffer a great deal, it is important that we find meaning in what we have endured. Without seeing meaning, a person can lose a sense of purpose, which can lead to hopelessness and a despairing conclusion that there is no meaning to life itself.

I once talked with a person who was highly skeptical of this forgiveness approach. She said to me, "But isn't this just playing games with ourselves? We make up a little fantasy tale that all things happen for a reason and then all is well." Her views challenged me until I realized that she was talking about finding a positive meaning in the injustice itself. What I had meant when talking with her was to try to find meaning in the *aftermath* of the injustice, in the suffering that takes place as you move through life once the injustice has occurred. I also meant what meaning she might be finding—again, not in the injustice itself—but in the suffering that is occurring even now, if the injustice continues and is unavoidable as part of her life for the moment. I was asking her what she has learned from the suffering itself as a way to heal and grow as a person.

There is a large difference between trying to find goodness in the badness of another person's actions and trying to see how *your own suffering has changed you in a positive way*. Finding meaning in your suffering can help you live well.

Example of Finding Meaning in Suffering

Consider one person's meaning in a dramatic case of grave suffering. Eva Moses Kor was one of the Jewish twins on whom Josef Mengele did his evil experiments in the Auschwitz concentration camp during World War II. In the film *Forgiving Dr. Mengele*, Mrs. Kor tells her story of survival and ultimate forgiveness of this notorious doctor, also known as the "Angel of Death." In describing her imprisonment as a child at Auschwitz, she said, "It is a place that I lived between life and death." Soon after her imprisonment in the concentration camp, young Eva was injected with a lethal drug so powerful that Mengele pronounced, after examining her, that she had only two weeks to live. "I refused to die," was her response.

Her meaning in what she was suffering in the immediate short run was to prove Mengele wrong and thus to do anything that she possibly could to survive. Her second meaning in her suffering was to survive for the sake of her twin sister, Miriam. She knew that if she, Eva, died, Mengele immediately would kill Miriam with an injection to the heart and then do a comparative autopsy on the two sisters. "I spoiled the experiment," was her understated conclusion. A third meaning in her suffering, a longer but still short-term goal, was to endure it so that she could be reunited with Miriam. A long-term goal from her suffering ultimately was to forgive this man who had no concern whatsoever for her life or the lives of those he condemned to the gas chamber. She willed her own survival against great odds, and she made it.

In this case, fiendish power met a fierce will to survive. Upon forgiving Mengele, she saw great meaning in what she had suffered. She has addressed many student groups, showing them a better way than carrying resentment through life. She opened a Holocaust museum in a small town in the United States. And she realizes that her suffering and subsequent forgiveness both have a meaning in challenging others to consider forgiving people for whatever injustices they are enduring. Her ultimate message is that forgiveness is stronger than Nazi power. And it has helped her to thrive. As you can imagine, Mrs. Kor is a controversial figure because not all who suffered as she did are ready to forgive. She realizes this, too, and makes the important point that she has for-given the Nazis in her name only, not on behalf of others. Each has his or her own choice to make. Each is free to find his or her own meaning in this atrocity or any injustice that comes. You, too, have the inner freedom to choose what meaning you find in what you have suffered.

When We See No Meaning in Our Suffering

Had Mrs. Kor found no meaning in the imprisonment, in the intended lethal injection, and in her loss of family, she easily could have died. Yet she did not because of a fierce will to overcome the injustice, hope for Miriam's life, and now hope that she can con-tribute compassion and forgiveness to other people.

Are you able to find meaning in what you have suffered? The consequences of walking through life with no sense of meaning in what you have endured or are enduring are too important for you not to strive toward meaning—a meaning that only you can discover.

From No Meaning to Meaning: Two Examples

Jeremiah, when I first met him, had no meaning in his life. He had struggled with psychological depression most of his adult life. He is now 45 years old, divorced, and his children are grown and gone. "I don't have a good relationship with my own children. I'm sick of that. No one really cares if I live or die!" he proclaimed to me. "I need love in my life, but it's gone. I have nothing to live for. I'm thinking of putting my documents in order and then killing myself. I am so tired of being depressed." I could see his despair and isolation. As we talked, he mentioned that there is a homeless person in his community with whom he does have a strong relationship. "We do get along great. He needs me." When I pointed out that his friend would be devastated by his (Jeremiah's) suicide, he looked at me with anger as if to say, "How dare you take away my plan."

But as Jeremiah imagined his friend, whom he met several days each week on a particular park bench, now devastated by his suicide, he burst into tears, finally realizing that he was about to do something that would profoundly withdraw love from a person who already is beaten down by life. Jeremiah could not bear the thought of adding this burden to his homeless friend, who relied on Jeremiah for emotional support. All of a sudden Jeremiah had meaning in his life: to bear his suffering for his friend, to survive, and to get better so that his friend would not have to endure the pain of sudden and unexplained loss. And, of course, the sudden loss of a valued friend through suicide has a much deeper impact on those left behind than does, say, passing away from cancer where there is no hint of withdrawing love from others. A reason to live, even just a short-term goal—these are part of finding meaning. Note that in this case, the meaning centered specifically on service love, the kind of love that uplifts others, even as the person carries his or her own pain.

Agatha, an 87-year-old widow, recently broke her arm. She had surgery and was now undergoing physical and occupational therapy to help her regain the use of her arm and to learn how to get around in her kitchen. The physical therapist noticed that she was not being compliant in doing her daily exercises. "If you do not do the exercises, you will not progress. If you do not progress, then I will not be able to come to visit you for physical rehab," the specialist explained to her.

It became apparent to the physical rehab specialist that Agatha had no meaning in her life. She therefore had no incentive to do the necessary work to get better. A psychologist then discovered that her parents had mistreated her when she was a child. There was much harsh criticism directed her way when she was young and a message that she had little inherent worth. For all of these years, Agatha had harbored deep resentment against her parents, undermining her ability to form meaningful and trusting relationships as an adult. As a result, she had remained single and with few friends for most of her life.

When the psychologist suggested that she consider forgiving her parents, at first she was hesitant. She did not want to put the energy into that when her arm was now taking most of her daily energy. When the psychologist explained that forgiving the parents was not a way to excuse them and that it could unburden her of her lifetime of resentment, she said she would give it a try. As she began learning about forgiveness, this activity itself became very meaningful to her, to such an extent that she began writing about her forgiveness experience—and these were published as small reflections in her church newspaper. Others, intrigued by her insights, began to contact her. Her small circle of friends began to widen, and she no longer felt a sense of deep isolation. Her energy improved and she started physical rehabilitation with a renewed vigor, eventually getting back the use of her arm. From seeing no meaning to life, forgiveness gave her meaning, friends, and a new arm.

Reminder 32:

Meaning gives hope to the suffering you have experienced and may ultimately bring joy into your life.

What Does "Finding Meaning" Really Mean?

As I hope you are beginning to see, your finding meaning in what you have suffered will aid you along life's path. But just what does it mean to *find meaning in suffering*?

To find meaning is to see that as one suffers, it is possible to develop short-term and even long-range goals in life. Some people, for example, begin to think about how to use their suffering as a means to cope in the here and now. Eventually, they realize that their suffering has altered their perspective regarding what is important in life, changing their long-range goals. Finding meaning in suffering is to develop a growth-producing answer to the "why" question.

One can find meaning through suffering in one's work. Perhaps the little annoyances will roll off now. Perhaps doing work that adds something of value to the world will draw you now that you have suffered.

Finding meaning in the pursuit of truth is yet another way of finding meaning after or while you suffer. When we are hurt by others who exert power over us, there is a tendency to blur the lines between what is the truth and what is a lie. Consider the suffering of the psychiatrist Viktor Frankl, who was in concentration camps in Germany and Poland during World War II. When Dr. Frankl was ordered to go on a march to do some slave work, I am sure that the soldiers controlling his behavior were convinced that they were doing the right thing. They likely had convinced themselves that those they had enslaved somehow deserved it. Dr. Frankl resisted their lies and consciously stood in the truth that what he was experiencing was unjust. One can become stronger by realizing that one's suffering has sharpened the mind to see what is right and what is wrong, even when others are trying to convince you otherwise.

Becoming motivated and resolved to be a good person is yet another way to find meaning in your suffering. People sometimes become motivated to be morally good because they now see the effects of not begin good in what they have suffered from others, who might have refused to be good. Growing in goodness can include working on being more resolute or strong inside and on being more loving and forgiving. In other words, you know down deep that you are developing and even thriving as a person, despite being stepped on by others who perhaps are expanding their own worlds through power seeking.

Appreciating beauty can be a strong and protective way of finding meaning in your suffering. The darkness of others' behavior can make one more attuned to the light, to the beauty that actually exists here and now. Appreciating beauty, taking it inside of you, may help you transcend your wounds and make them more bearable. Eventually, as you forgive, you may find beauty in forgiveness itself.

When you feel like you have been pressed down by others, a new meaning can emerge that you now want to serve others, to help them *up* when they have been pressed down. Your compassion motivates you to help.

Finally, growth in understanding and appreciating your particular faith, if you have one, may be a new avenue of finding meaning in your life. C. S. Lewis made this point in his book *The Problem of Pain*, after he lost his wife to illness. His faith was not diminished by the pain; instead he used it as an opportunity to explore his faith more deeply. As people forgive, they realize that they need to be forgiven, which furthers the insight that, once forgiven, it is good to forgive. The combination of being forgiven and then forgiving others makes possible genuine and healthy reconciliation. To suffer well, then, is to hope for a better future for those who have been unfair to you.

Reminder 33:

To find meaning in what you have suffered is a path out of discouragement and despair and into greater hope.

What Finding Meaning in Suffering Is *Not*

When you find meaning in your life and in the suffering that you endured, you are *not* doing any of the following:

- You are not denying anger, grief, or disappointment because of what happened to you. It did happen and your negative response is completely appropriate. To find meaning is not to put the pillow over your head and hope the pain goes away.

• When you find meaning, you are not playing games with yourself by saying, "Oh, well, I can just make the best of what happened to me." Yes, you *can* make the best of what happened, but if this is the meaning you find in what you have suffered, you are unlikely to address the woundedness inside of you—which this journey with our eight keys is all about. The "Oh, well" approach is passive. Healing woundedness requires an active approach to the pain.

• When you find meaning, you are not sugarcoating the injustice and distorting reality by saying, "All things happen for good reasons, so I will try to see the good in what was done to me." But maybe there was not anything good to be found in the injustice itself. What you learn from it will have goodness, but the event itself? It is not necessary, or even recommended, to find goodness in the injustice you experienced.

Finding *Your* Meaning in What You Have Suffered

So what meaning do you see in what you are suffering or have suffered? This is not an easy question to answer because there can be so many different answers, as we have seen above. For Mrs. Kor, at least in the short run, her meaning was not to let the suffering kill her. For another who is struggling in a partner relationship, it might be to learn that she, too, is imperfect and so she will be more tolerant with her imperfect partner. For yet another who is in a boring job, the person uses his suffering to carefully think through what his career priorities are and to devise concrete steps for realizing them.

In other words, there is no rulebook that tells us exactly what meaning we will find in our suffering. If I were to give an answer, it would be that we are to use our suffering to become more loving and then to pass that love to others. Finding a positive meaning, in and of itself, is helpful to healing whether or not you agree with me at this point on the specific meaning for you.

In this fifth room with the fifth key, you now have the task to figure out what *your* meaning is for what you have suffered. How has this suffering changed you? What new directions in your life will you take because you have suffered in this particular way?

As a first step in figuring out the meaning for your suffering, let's take a little time to examine some other people's responses to these questions of finding meaning in suffering. The following sections present examples of courageous people who have struggled toward meaning in the aftermath of deep injustices against them. After considering these examples, it will then be your turn to uncover your specific meaning(s).

Finding Meaning in Beauty

Josiah, 29 years old, is currently in a hospital bed in his home. He is there because an inebriated person smashed into his car, which overturned. He now has paraplegia, recovering as best he can. He feels imprisoned by his nonfunctioning legs. The prison, as you can imagine, is a challenge. To date, he has spent six months in this bed recovering from injuries.

He fights the temptation to despair by taking in the beauty of the open countryside and brook in back of his home whenever he is out in the yard with family members. Josiah has begun learning how to paint, and his goal is to capture the beauty of the countryside on canvas. The painted landscape will be a symbol of his forgiving—peaceful, quiet, and helpful to his family and to him. In Josiah's own words: "I can let the consequences of the driver's actions kill me, or I can go to a higher place—and the incredible countryside leads me there. It reminds me of all that is good in the world and so it gives me the strength to go on. The car accident has imprisoned my body for now, but not my soul. No act of negligence will ever be able to touch me at my core of who I am now."

Finding Meaning in Forgiveness Itself

Samantha, 34 years old and separated from her husband because of physical abuse against her, at first thought that forgiveness was a dangerous thing. I recall her piercing eyes when I first brought up the topic. She explained to me that her husband is under court order not to come within a certain distance of her for her own safety. When she heard the word *forgiveness*, she immediately thought of a mindless and dangerous reconciliation with the man who has beaten her more times than she cares to remember. She was angry with me for even using the word, which I had not yet suggested to her as a way to heal emotionally.

After talking about what forgiveness is and is not for a long time, she finally came around to see that forgiveness is a *protection for her heart*, not a behavioral move that puts her in danger. She embraced the idea, began to forgive her husband, and it changed her life. "I need this topic and I need it in my heart," she said. "I do not know of another way to get rid of the rage other than to forgive him. It is kind of scary to think of my being trapped for the rest of my life with the boiling rage that I used to feel for him. I think I can go on now with greater confidence. When the anger comes, I now have a response to it."

Forgiveness brought meaning because it showed Samantha that she could overcome her anger, which had unsettled her because of its intensity. Her meaning for now is to use forgiveness as a way to quiet her inner rage and so to slowly begin to put her life back together.

Finding Meaning in Service to Others

Melissa, a 21-year-old immigrant to the United States from Australia, has had a history of arguments with her mother, and so she decided to immigrate to escape the conflict. Her adjustment in the new land has not been easy. She had trouble finding work and in making friends. She felt isolated and thought about returning to Australia, but each time she considered this, she thought of the conflicts with her mother, which invariably increased her stress level. Trying to adjust to the new land for her was the better choice at this point.

In her pain, Melissa began to be more sensitive to other people's pain. She saw a niche that she could enter in her community. She received training in early childhood education and began her career as a teacher's assistant in the classroom. Her service to children helped her to put her own pain in perspective. She did not minimize the conflict in her own childhood, and she kept to the truth that she still has the challenge of forgiving and reconciling with her mother. At the same time, she was able to put her own pain into good service to the children, some of whom also were carrying great pain from conflict in their homes. Melissa knows what it is like to grow up with conflict, and so she is particularly patient and gentle with these children. She gives them love that helps their hurting hearts, and in the giving, she is experiencing emotional healing.

In looking back on her life, Melissa thinks that it was the continual arguments with her mother that helped her to find the meaning in her suffering by wanting to be in service to children. She loves her job and is deeply fulfilled by it. Even when other teachers and assistants complain about the children, she sees more deeply than that. She sees hurting hearts where others just see behaviors in need of correction. Melissa is seeing with clearer vision because of the wounds that entered her heart years ago and that she currently is working on healing.

Exercises for Finding Meaning in Your Own Suffering

If you are ready to explore the meaning in what you have suffered, review the various forms of meaning previously covered in this chapter and consider which of these apply directly to you. The exercises here do not prepare you to engage in specific behaviors to achieve the goals. These exercises are intended only to give you insight. Insight is needed first, and then action, which we take up with Key 8.

Exercise #1: Finding Meaning in Your Short-Term Goals

Write down, either on paper or electronically, your answers to the following questions:

Mrs. Kor's immediate goal was to stay alive. Do you have a goal of keeping your heart alive after what you have suffered from another person's injustice toward you? Even if your body is very much alive, your heart—the center of your love, enthusiasm, and passion for life—may be dying. Is it? If so, what is your immediate goal for reenergizing your heart?

Exercise #2: Finding Meaning in Crafting Long-Range Goals

Your priorities in life might have changed because of this journey of suffering you have been on. Write down what used to seem very important to you, which now seems kind of trivial, unimportant, not really contributing to your and others' happiness. Be specific here so you know what to let go in your life.

What is one response to the suffering that you now see as important in preserving your humanity in the long run? In other words, what do you need in your life so that serious injustice does not defeat you?

What used to seem trivial and unimportant to you that now seems very important? Again, try to name whatever this is. What will help to make you whole again? Your answer could form the basis of new actions in your life, a theme we take up with Key 8.

Exercise #3: Finding Meaning in Your Work

How has suffering changed your view of work and the workplace? If you are a homemaker, how has the suffering changed your view of how to serve in the home? As in the above exercise, consider what used to seem so vitally important that now seems kind of trivial and unimportant. Conversely, does what used to seem somewhat unimportant to you now seem vital to what you do?

Reminder 34:

As you make new goals in light of what you have suffered, you are adding new meaning to your life.

Exercise #4: Finding Meaning through Standing in the Truth

It was Aristotle, over 2,000 years ago, who gave us the most elegant definition of the truth: "to say of what is that it is and to say of that which is not that it is not." Were you treated unjustly? Say of what is that it is: "I was treated unjustly."

Are you now at risk for a bitter heart if you do not do heart surgery for your emotional healing? Say of what is that it is: "I now have to be careful because the injustice has challenged the health of my heart. I am aware of this and my suffering shows this to me."

Is the other right (such as saying there was no injustice) because she (or he) says she is right? Say of that which is not that it is not: "No, I stand in the truth that I was treated unjustly and I will not back off from that, even if someone tries to contradict me. I know how to see now, and I will not back down from this new way of seeing injustice clearly." Of course, you also need balance here. If you have been in denial and have distorted the other's actions, then this is not standing in the truth. In such a case, the truth would be this: "I was mistaken. The other person was not unjust as I had first thought."

Reminder 35:

Your suffering can help you to see the truth about what is just and unjust.

Exercise #5: Finding Meaning in Being Good

Are you a good person despite what has happened to you? Let your suffering help you see the truth: "I am a good person no matter what others say about me or do to me." How can your suffering increase your resolve to be good to others? Think for a minute about how the other person's unfairness has affected you. Do you want that kind of suffering now for others because of your unwillingness to be morally good?

Reminder 36:

Your suffering can help you realize that you will not let the badness in this world rob you of your goodness . . . for the good of others.

Exercise #6: Finding Meaning in the Truth that You Are Good Despite Your Suffering

We tend to lose confidence and appreciation of ourselves when we are deeply wounded by others. Yet when we take a closer look, we see differently and more clearly. Look at what you have suffered and endured. Does a weak and worthless person face suffering like this? Your suffering shows you how you persevere despite perhaps feeling like you have been crushed by another's actions. What does your going through this suffering, then, tell you about . . . you?

Reminder 37:

Your suffering has not been for nothing. It can make you more attuned to the goodness within you.

Exercise #7: Finding Meaning in Strengthening Your Inner Resolve

Do you think that some people who hurt others actually like to see those people suffer? Sometimes those who are very, very angry can and do derive a certain pleasure in inflicting their pain onto others. If your abuser fits this description, don't give him or her that satisfaction. Instead, try to find this meaning in how you have suffered. Some people find it helpful to make resolutions, such as the following:

"I will work on becoming stronger internally by standing up to the injustice."

"I will work on maintaining an inner calm, a firmness in not letting meanness and cruelty destroy me."

"I will learn a lesson from Mrs. Kor and cultivate a strong and good will in the face of what I am suffering."

"There is too much suffering in this world, and so I re-solve to put goodness into it."

This challenge can give great meaning to your suffering as you realize that you are much stronger than you had realized.

Reminder 38:

Your suffering can be a means of making you stronger.

Exercise #8: Finding Meaning in Beauty

Too often the deep healing through beauty remains unseen by too many in the hurry-up, make-a-buck modern world. Yet, true beauty has a way of deeply satisfying the human heart. People know beauty when they see it.

Beauty, when you let it, extends a hand to you from above the pit and beckons you to rise out of it for something better. Beauty lifts the spirit and transcends all of the darkness and unfairness that you have experienced in your life. Beauty, in other words, helps to heal you.

People find meaning in their suffering when they realize that it has softened their hearts to letting in something bigger than themselves. Dr. Frankl relates one incident during his time in a concentration camp in which he and his fellow prisoners would deliberately admire the beauty of the mountains when they were about to go on a forced march or do outside slave labor. Focusing on experiencing the beauty of the mountains, deep down inside of them, was a stronger force affecting their emotions than was the pain of the march and the exhaustion of the labor. They were choosing to turn their attention toward something that would lift their hearts amidst the ugliest of conditions. Beauty gave them meaning and stoked their will to live because they realized, deep down, that there is more to this life than the pains of a particular day.

Reminder 39:

If you choose, you will begin today to see beauty rather than only the darkness and you will never let the darkness win.

Here is another story from that same era. Anne Frank, a Jewish girl, began to make notes in a diary on her 13th birthday to describe her experience as the Nazis marched through her town, Amsterdam. Her family had gone into hiding in a building where her father worked. Eventually, they were caught and she and her sister, Margo, were transferred to a concentration camp in Germany, where Anne died of typhus in 1945. Her diary was eventually found by her father and published as *The Diary of a Young Girl*. Despite the fear of being in hiding, the breakup of her family, and the deportation to a concentration camp, she wrote this: "Think of all the beauty still left around you and be happy." All of the ugliness and hatred did not defeat her. She held to the beauty in her heart.

When we are weighed down by pain, we tend to focus only on the pain and not on the beauty of the world. But that tendency can be changed if you choose to change your focus. You are more than your pain. You are more than your scars. You are more than your imperfections—and so is the one who has hurt you. Reflect on the idea that you yourself are beautiful, despite all you have been through. Do you think that all of Anne Frank's suffering diminished her beauty? Or did it increase her beauty? Think carefully about the following thoughts from Victoria Moran: "To the people who love you, you are beautiful already. This is not because they're blind to your shortcomings but because they so clearly see your soul. Your shortcomings then dim by comparison. The people who care about you are willing to let you be imperfect and beautiful, too."

Your suffering has given you a softer heart, and that means that you are becoming more beautiful inwardly. Of course, I am not encouraging you to seek more suffering so that your inner beauty further emerges. Rather, let the challenges in your life be a new opportunity to bring out that beauty in you.

Reminder 40:

Your inner qualities of beauty are brought forth by your suffering.

Now to our exercise. Over the next week, try to be aware of at least four instances of beauty: one, involving physical scenery; another, a person in what he or she is doing, his or her personality, a look toward you; a third, a created work of art such as a painting, a musical composition, the written word; and last, reflect on the possibility that forgiveness itself is beautiful. Ask yourself each time: "Am I more aware of beauty now that I have suffered deeply? If so, who am I now becoming as a person?"

Exercise #9: Finding Meaning in Service to Others

Are you feeling strong enough at this point to ask, "What can I do for others? How can I be of service to those who have hurting hearts?" The point here is not to change jobs or to work full time at a service agency that offers meals to those suffering on the streets (although that would be great if this is what you see as your vocation to others now), nor is it to add many more hours to what is probably already a full workload. The point is to begin to take advantage of those moments when you can extend the hand of mercy to another hurting person: a smile, a pat on the back, a word of encouragement. Even small gestures can be acts of service to others.

Try to see the wounded hearts of others and then try to do something, no matter how seemingly small the world tells you that it is, to help heal that heart. You will find that in attempting to heal others' hearts, your own heart begins to heal a little more.

Reminder 41:

As you give service to others with wounded hearts, your heart begins to heal.

Exercise #10: Finding Meaning in Forgiveness and in Being Forgiven

As you find that you are becoming more whole as a person in your forgiveness of those who have hurt you, does this process of forgiving impart meaning to your suffering? After all, without that suffering, you never would have discovered the truth, goodness, and beauty of forgiveness. You would not be armed against power that can damage your heart. Your suffering has made you a wiser person regarding what forgiveness is and how it is practiced. Take some time now to write out your thoughts to these questions:

- How has your suffering helped you to become a more forgiving person?
- How has your suffering helped you to more readily seek forgiveness from those you have hurt?

Reminder 42:

Suffering can add to your knowledge of what forgiveness is. Suffering can aid you in becoming a more forgiving person and in seeking forgiveness from others.

Exercise #11: Finding Meaning in Faith

If you are a member of a particular religion, then you have an opportunity to find meaning in suffering through your faith in those beliefs. Here are just a few examples. In Buddhism (which some consider a faith, whereas others consider it more of a philosophy of life) the challenge is to rise above or transcend the anger and suffering. Suffering offers the opportunity to practice nonattachment to worldly interactions and values that end up bringing dissatisfaction and pain. In the Hindu approach, people are taught to have mercy on those who have made them suffer. Within the Jewish tradition is the exhortation to love one's neighbor as one loves the self and to imitate God, who is mercy. In Christianity, the believer has a model in Jesus Christ, who also preached the virtue of loving one's neighbor as oneself, and who suffered unjustly out of love for others and now the task is to imitate and unite in love with the one who first sacrificed for humankind. In the Muslim faith, the believer reads in the Koran that God is all loving and forgiving. The challenge, as in Judaism and Christianity, is to imitate this characteristic.

So, then, to our questions directed to people who have a faith or set of religious convictions.

- What does your particular faith have to say about suffering?
- What are the challenges in this teaching for you personally?
- Can you see how your faith is asking you to grow as a person?

Again, try to be specific in answering just how you are supposed to be growing and how you are actually growing as you listen to the advice from your faith.

Reminder 43:

Try to see what your faith tradition says about suffering and the overcoming of suffering as an opportunity for you to grow as a person.

Questions about Finding Meaning in Suffering

Question 1

"Can I find more than just one meaning in my suffering? I have a few meanings, but it's getting a little confusing for me trying to figure out which meaning really explains my suffering."

Not only might you have more than one meaning to consider right now but also you will likely add more meanings as you continue our journey. Some meanings may become less important over time, whereas others will emerge as vital for you. I suggest for now, to lessen your confusion, that you list the top three meanings from the set of exercises we just completed. Make those your focus for now and stay open to additions and changes as you walk this path of forgiveness.

Question 2

"Could I get to a point that I find a certain meaning as a way to rationalize going back to an unhealthy relationship?"

Yes, this can happen. For example, someone might falsely conclude this: "Well, I'm learning a lot from what I've suffered, so the more I suffer . . . the more I will learn. Therefore, it is okay not to protect myself as I go back to an unhealthy and damaging relationship for the other and for me."

Note that I used the word *falsely* in the preceding paragraph. So, yes, this can happen, but it definitely should not. When it does happen, it is occurring from a position of confusion, not clarity. As you see with clearer vision, you will see that you should not get out of balance with how you deal with suffering by finding meaning. Anything good in this world can be distorted to such a degree that it no longer is what it started out to be, and its fruit is no longer what it should be. So be aware of extreme views that can distort what suffering is and the meaning behind it. One way to avoid this false move toward finding meaning in suffering is to ask yourself: Am I putting myself in danger and somehow justifying this as a way to find meaning and grow as a person? If the answer is yes, then first please avoid the danger and then reassess how to find meaning without seeking suffering.

Question 3

"Have you ever worked with someone who found no meaning in the suffering or in forgiveness itself? If so, how did you handle that?"

Yes, I have worked with people who have found no meaning in their suffering or in forgiveness itself, but this usually happens at the beginning of the journey and not at the halfway point or beyond. When this does happen, I try to show the person our forgiveness map, the eight keys we are discussing in this book. As people see that there is more to forgiveness than what they are seeing and experiencing that particular day, they tend to take the longer view of it and find the patience to develop clearer vision over time. This overview of the journey gives those initially struggling both hope and a challenge to keep on the forgiveness path and not give up because today it feels hopeless. Seeing beyond today helps people penetrate the darkness of their immediate moment.

Question 4

"What is the difference between finding meaning in suffering and finding a new purpose as a result of the suffering?"

To find meaning is to gain an insight in the mind. It is an inner process. Finding a new purpose, although it originates as a set of ideas in the mind, flows out to actual behaviors and relationships with others. The purpose is what someone actually plans to do and actually does once the meaning is in clearer focus.

Question 5

"How can I find meaning when the other person just keeps up the injustice like a freight train coming my way?"

It is harder to think when we are being emotionally beaten by others. Nevertheless, when others keep coming at us with injustice, it is imperative that we work even harder to find the meaning in what we are enduring because we must not be overcome by another's cruelty. Take time, when you are away from this person, to practice forgiveness so that your emotions are quieter, and from that position keep asking yourself the questions:

"What am I learning from this?"

"How can I protect myself in the short run so that I am not overwhelmed?"

"How can I put what I am learning into action so that this injustice ends?"

Bear in mind that forgiveness and justice "grow up" together. This is not a matter of one or the other but of taking them *both* along as you solve the problem and work toward emotional healing.

Reminder 44:

Forgiveness and justice "grow up" together, so never toss either one aside.

Question 6

"I disagree with those who say that finding meaning reduces suffering. It seems to me that as a person accumulates a lot of suffering in life, the pain does not go down. It goes up. Sure, we can find meaning in that, but how can you say it *reduces* the suffering?"

The immediate answer is this: Yes, suffering can go up. In the long view, however, as you fight for your well-being through the practice of forgiveness, as described in this book, the suffering is likely to start going down for you. This process takes time, motivation, and practice. Try not to let today's suffering be your final word on how far you will progress in conquering the effects of that suffering. How you are feeling today need not be your permanent state.

Reminder 45:

When suffering intensifies, know that this is not your final state. Forgiveness eventually leads to a reduction in the internally felt suffering and in the negative aftereffects of that suffering.

Question 7

"As I try to reduce my suffering by finding meaning in it, I still find myself wanting the one who hurt me to suffer. Does this mean that I am not advancing as a forgiver?"

First, even asking such a question shows your motivation to forgive. Try to think of your forgiveness as falling along a continuum, from having only a glimmer of forgiveness to having a surprising love for the one who did not love you. You are not at the "surprising love" end of the continuum yet. Welcome to the club, as they say. We all struggle with forgiveness; it truly is a journey of growth that takes time and effort, so do not condemn yourself for getting angry all over again with a person who has hurt you. You recognize the anger (in this case, as a kind of revenge), and as you recognize this, start from the beginning of Key 4 and forgive afresh. As you keep practicing forgiveness, the thoughts of revenge will fade. Be gentle with yourself as this process unfolds.

Question 8

"Are there typical kinds of meanings that you see people who are new at forgiving express, compared to the meanings you see expressed by those who have forgiven many people over many years?"

Yes, there is a considerable difference. For those who are new at forgiving, the immediate meaning tends to be something like this: "I know that I have to find a way to emotionally heal from this, and so I will work on these short-term plans to heal my wounded heart."

Over time, people tend to find meaning in what they can give to other people—which may include the ones who were hurtful as well as a much wider circle of people who are part of this suffering person's world. They find meaning in giving, in other words.

Question 9

"All of your examples of finding meaning are positive—seeing beauty, serving others, for example. But what if my meaning is that I have discovered something negative about myself, that I am too selfish as a person? Will this hinder my ability to forgive?"

This insight will hinder your ability to forgive if you stop right there and do not keep going on the forgiveness path. Seeing something negative in yourself offers a great opportunity for you to *do* something about that quality. That *is* a new meaning. As you now want to correct something within you, which is directly implied in your question, you just changed meaning from "I see that I am deficient" to "I commit to working out of that, now that I see it." Your question is a transition to what you are calling an example of something "positive": that is, to grow in character.

Question 10

"I am actually afraid to find my meaning in suffering because I do not want to look suffering in the eye. What do you suggest in a case like this?"

Many people are afraid to examine their own degree of suffering or even their degree of anger because they see no solution once they "look suffering in the eye" (or anger). However, forgiveness itself provides a strong resolution to suffering and anger, so it is all right for you to stand in the truth of seeing your suffering as well as your level of anger. Forgiveness is your safety net. As you see that suffering, bolstered by the confidence that forgiveness gives you, then try to discern what meaning this suffering has for you. The result is likely to be a significant reduction in that suffering.

Reminder 46:

You need not fear "looking suffering in the eye" because forgiveness is a safety net for you. Forgiveness can protect you from the heart-wounds of suffering and make you stronger.

Final Exercises to Strengthen Your Ability to Find Meaning in Suffering

Three final exercises are offered to further strengthen your use of this key.

Exercise #12: Daily Statements

Take the time to read and reflect on the following daily statements or affirmations, intended to make the search for meaning important for you as you continue this journey of life:

> "As I find meaning in my suffering, it helps me to stand up to the injustice that happened to me."
> "I will never give into others' cruelty and meanness with despair because then injustice wins."
> "I will continue to develop the mind of forgiveness despite the suffering."

Exercise #13: Ordering the Meanings

Of the 11 meanings to suffering discussed in this chapter, which one is the best for you right now? Which is the second best? Rank the following 11 meanings in order of importance to you, then deliberately focus on the top three meanings each day:

> Meaning 1. Forming strong short-term goals that help me cope in the short run.
> Meaning 2. Forming worthwhile long-range goals that could be deeply satisfying.

Meaning 3. Rethinking how I should approach the world of work.

Meaning 4. Standing in the truth no matter what.

Meaning 5. Developing a greater appreciation of what it means to be good.

Meaning 6. Not losing sight of the thought that I am good, despite all of the suffering.

Meaning 7. Becoming more resolute in knowing that I must be good because there is too much suffering in the world.

Meaning 8. Developing a much deeper appreciation of beauty.

Meaning 9. Realizing that service to others is very rewarding.

Meaning 10. Learning about forgiving and seeking forgiveness as a new approach to life.

Meaning 11. Learning more about the subtleties of my particular faith because of what I have suffered.

Exercise #14: Reassessing Your Forgiveness Fitness

In Key 4, I reminded you that you are becoming increasingly forgivingly fit and that you have to keep at it to maintain the fitness. How are you doing on becoming more forgivingly fit at this point? Are you feeling less fit, about the same, or fitter compared to your self-assessment in the previous chapter? If you are feeling less fit, I think the cause might be fatigue. Take a break, refresh. There is time to increase your fitness; take the long-term view and feel hopeful. If you are about the same level of fitness, then stay at it and grow further. If you are feeling more forgivingly fit, then enjoy that feeling and reach for more. It is exhilarating to use fitness to increase that fitness, to become fitter still—this time, using Key 6.

KEY 6

WHEN IT'S HARD TO FORGIVE

Today I Will Stand
I have been hurt and so I will stand . . .
 not with a clenched fist and tightened jaw
 not to seek or gain power over my injurer
 not to defy or to threaten.
Today I will stand . . .
 with love
 with mercy
 and with understanding
 and I will not give up.

Forgiveness is always hard when we are dealing with deep injustices from others. After all, to extend mercy to anyone who has not had mercy on you is a gift hard to give. Sometimes the forgiving gets especially difficult to give. It becomes an agony of trying to give the gift of understanding and compassion. I have known people who refuse to use the word *forgiveness* because it just makes them so angry. They are not yet ready to offer mercy. And that is okay. We all have our own timelines for when we can be merciful. The fact that you have reached this far in the book shows that you are motivated to forgive. At the same time, your reading this chapter might suggest that you have hit a rut in your road and may be about to stumble on the forgiveness journey. Let's sidestep that rut with Key 6 and consider how to proceed . . . "When It's Hard to Forgive."

 Taking up this key might seem a little intimidating because we are talking about the *really* hard aspects of forgiveness. Perhaps you have some apprehension or even some fear at this point. Have you encountered anything in Keys 1 through 5 that help you with apprehension or fear? You have met many challenges so far. Reflect on those achievements as a way to boost your confidence now.

Stories of Tough Forgiveness

As in the previous chapters, we'll begin here by considering some examples where forgiving was exceedingly hard to do.

A Case of Patience and Time

When Suzanne Freedman and I did our scientific study with incest survivors and forgiveness (described in Key 1), as you can imagine, the process toward wholeness was very difficult for each participant. As mentioned, each took about 14 months to forgive. Had any one of them assessed their progress, say, at the beginning of the fifth month or even the eighth month, they might have concluded that they were not there yet and may even have doubted that they would ever experience the forgiveness for which they were searching. And yet they did, all of them. I mention this example as a further encouragement to you.

One of the incest survivors, upon tapping into forgiveness for her father, actually helped with his care while he was dying in the hospital. She had come to see him as possessing inherent worth, not because of what he did, of course. She saw with clearer vision by using a wide-angle lens and seeing that he had good qualities, despite the psychological sickness that had led to his actions. When looking back on her own situation, she said that she was glad to have forgiven her father because now, upon his passing, she had only mourning to confront, and her heart was soft enough to mourn. She said that, had she stayed unforgiving, then her emotions would be blending mourning or sadness and rage. That combination would have been too much for her, in her own view. In the case of the incest survivors, effort and patience, along with following the advice in our Keys 4 and 5 over 14 months, proved to be deciding factors for these individuals in meeting the challenge of when it is hard to forgive.

A Case of a Strong Will and Bearing the Pain

In another case, Aaron's wife of three years had two affairs with two different men. He was so upset that he could not use the word *forgiveness*. Words such as *acceptance, understanding,* and *giving it over to a higher power* worked for him, but not *forgiveness* or even *mercy.* Over time, Aaron stayed on a forgiveness path (although he did not call it that) through his strong will to try to respect his wife, despite the affairs. By using this word *respect,* he did not condone her actions, but instead he willed himself to see that she had emotional troubles and that he chose, by his strong will, to accept her as a person, even though he could no longer accept her in the specific role of wife.

Eventually, Aaron had the insight that despite his continuing anger, he had to bear the pain of what had happened so that he did not pass that pain onto his growing son, whom he now was raising by himself. If he did not bear this pain, he might have displaced his anger onto his child. He, of course, wanted to help his son grow in as healthy a way as possible, and so he never condemned his wife to his family. He watched his temper and did not get overly angry when his son misbehaved. His strong will and his determination to bear the pain for his son were part of the forgiveness process for Aaron, even though he could never use the word.

A Case of Continual Forgiveness Practice
with Easier Offenses

Serika, a 35-year-old architect, was having a very difficult time forgiving her employer for laying her off with one week notice even though she had been a productive member of the company for over four years. Her faithfulness to the boss had been met with what she believed to be insensitivity and betrayal. No matter how hard she tried, she could not rid herself of burning resentment toward him. She had repeated nightmares about the job and the way she was treated for over three months.

Serika decided that she was not forgivingly fit enough to forgive her boss yet, so she started to do more of what I call "forgiveness practice" with others who have offended her much less. For example, she would forgive her own children daily when they would misbehave. She practiced forgiving her brother for insensitive, rude comments he made to her when she was an adolescent. It was much easier for her to see the inherent worth of her own children and her brother than it was for her to see this worth in her boss.

After about one month of this kind of practice, she started to transfer her learning about inherent worth to her boss. She discovered that now she could make the progress that she was seeking all along. She still concluded that he was an ineffective boss, but that he also was a person, an imperfect person, who had good qualities. For example, he donated some of the company's funds to local charities, not to receive publicity but instead because he saw this as a good thing to do. She eventually forgave him and moved on with her career.

In each of these cases, it was hard for the person to forgive. Each uses a little different approach, yet all were successful in shedding the resentment and becoming emotionally healthier people.

Exercises to Protect Your Emotional Health

You also need to protect your emotional health. Let's start by examining some important issues for you to consider when it is particularly difficult to offer forgiveness to someone who has deeply offended you.

Exercise #1: First and Foremost, Guard Who You Are

First you need to change your view of who you are as a person if you have been stuck in unforgiveness and are discouraged. The power perspective will tell you that you are less than you should be if your loved ones reject you. Do not listen to the voice of power. It is all too easy to condemn yourself when others first condemn you. Try to counter that power perspective starting now. Who are you as a person? You are someone who has inherent worth even when you struggle in life. You are someone who is special, unique, and irreplaceable even if you have unhealthy anger in your heart. You are *not* a failure at forgiveness. Remember that forgiveness is a process that takes time and patience and determination. Try not to be harsh on yourself if you are struggling with this process. How you are doing in this process today is not an indication of where you will be in this process one month from now. Who are you?

Reminder 47:

Despite being hurt by another, you can continue to realize that you are a person of great worth and that this worth cannot be taken away from you.

Exercise #2: Take the Long Perspective

Now think about one time in your childhood when you had what seemed to be a serious disagreement with a friend. At the time, did it seem like this breach would last forever? Did it? How long did it take to either reconcile or to find a new friend? Time has a way of changing our circumstances. This is not to advocate a kind of passive approach to life here—such as, "Oh, I'll just wait it out and not bother to exert any effort." That is not the point. The point is to take a long perspective so that you can see beyond the next hill to a place that is more settled and the pain is not so great. You already saw in your childhood that conflicts end. And the consequences of those conflicts (feeling sad or angry) also end. Why should that same process of change not also apply now? Try to see your circumstance, as realistically as you can, one month from now. Try to see your circumstance six months from now. Try to see yourself two years from now. Will you be the same person? Will you respond to injustices in the exact same way as you did three months ago? Probably not. You will likely be able to meet challenges with greater strength and wisdom as you continue on the forgiveness journey.

Reminder 48:

When you take a long perspective on your troubles, you see that you will be at a different point in your life one year from now.

Exercise #3: Be Gentle with Yourself

Guarding against your own false accusations against yourself is very important. At the same time, also add the practice of being gentle with yourself. By this I mean, try to foster a sense of quiet within, an inner acceptance of yourself. Try to respond to yourself as you would to someone whom you love deeply. Allow yourself to be imperfect and when you are, guard against a harsh inner voice that condemns. Because you have been wounded, you need that sense of self-acceptance in all aspects of your life right now.

The next time you make an error, be aware of how you are talking to yourself internally. Check to see if you are using the inner whip against yourself and then stop this immediately. Instead, try saying something like this to yourself: "I'm wounded inside. I don't need another wound, especially one that is inflicted from within. It is time to be gentle with myself."

Exercise #4: Surround Yourself as Best You Can with Good and Wise People

Who will support you in your woundedness? As we know, not everyone will. The point is not to set aside your interactions with those who do not see your wounds. Instead, consider asking yourself this: "Who actually sees my wounds and cares enough to be a part of the healing process?" The person might or might not be your therapist. Either way, become particularly aware of those people who have the patience to allow you time to heal in your own way, who stand with you and support your efforts to heal from the injustices you have experienced.

Try to name at least one person, and then a second person, who can do this for you or is already in this role. Within the next week, try to make contact with him or her. You do not even have to mention your woundedness. Sometimes it is enough just to be with others who simply know you are wounded and want to give you time to heal.

Exercise #5: Seek Professional Help if Necessary

If you think that your emotions are getting in the way of your functioning effectively, then consider two questions:

- Are these disruptive emotions with you most of the day?
- If so, how long have these emotions been affecting your functioning?

If you are experiencing this kind of disrupted daily life for two or more weeks, then it may be time for you to consider seeking professional help in dealing with your emotions.

There is a stereotype of seeking professional help that is

incorrect. The stereotype is that you must be "out of your mind" in a serious way if you have to consult with a psychiatrist, a clinical psychologist, or other mental health professional. The stereotype could prevent you from getting the help you need. Those who seek professional help are courageous. And this help need not be for a long duration, depending on your circumstances. Think of it this way: All of the people who might be in the waiting room are there because of a wounded heart. And here is another perspective: Your therapist may have sought professional help at some point for a wounded heart. So take courage in hand and join others who are wounded and in need of a little extra help.

More Specific Exercises to Forgive Those Who Are Hard to Forgive

It is time now to focus the exercises specifically on the forgiveness process. Do not expect that each of the exercises that follow will fit your particular situation. If you find one or more of these exercises unhelpful, then just skip it and go on to the next. If, on the other hand, you find an exercise that is particularly helpful for you, then make note of it and try to practice it daily until you are on track to forgive the person to whom you find it hard to offer your mercy and compassion.

Exercise #6: Humility

The 19th-century German philosopher Friedrich Nietzsche had disdain for this virtue, humility. He called it "a monkish virtue," and he was not exactly enamored of monks. Nietzsche's disdain of humility is no surprise, given that he coined the term *will to power* to describe what he saw as an innate human tendency to seek power over others and over nature. He said that power is about pushing others out of the way to claim more space, opportunity, and things in this world for the self. Which of these worldviews do you think he would choose: power or love?

Nietzsche was viewing humility through his lens of power. If, on the other hand, we view humility through the lens of love, what do we see? We see that humility is not a submissive stance of constantly putting oneself down. Instead, it is a realistic assessment of who we are as persons. We share personhood with all others. Therefore, you are not superior as a person to others. Sure, you may be a better tennis player than others or make more money, but when you look at personhood, we are all the same. We all need love and respect and mercy. Humility says, "I am not worse or better as a person than anyone else." Humility does not demand. It does not threaten. Humility takes its turn and allows others to take their turn.

A definition of humility that I recently read referred to it as a low view of one's own importance. Is that what humility is? I don't think so. Humility is not a distorted view of one's importance but a realistic assessment. If I am not a good tennis player, then the admission of this is humble. If, on the other hand, I say that I am less of a person than others, then this is a distortion and not a realistic assessment at all.

So now to our exercise. Who is this person who is hard to forgive? Is he or she a person who is less of a person because of what happened? He or she may have character defects in need of improvement. Do you have character defects in need of improvement? Look at the question with the clearer vision of humility and try to give a realistic assessment.

Injustice happens to every person, and every person at one time or another is unjust to others. You share this with the one who hurt you.

If you are feeling superior to the person who hurt you, are you able to widen that perception to see each of you as possessing the same inherent worth?

Does your struggle to forgive make you an inferior person? Even if you need more forgiveness practice, this does not diminish your personhood one little bit. Do you see that?

Try three times a day this wording, or something similar that you compose in your own words: "The one who hurt me and I share a common humanity. If we have an opportunity to talk about what happened, I will not make myself feel superior to him [her] in any way by what I say. I will be truthful but at the same time try to avoid the distortions of superiority or inferiority as persons."

Humility will help you stay on track with these statements.

Exercise #7: Courage

If you had to choose only four moral virtues to live by, what would they be? Would you include courage as one of the four? Socrates did, over 2,000 years ago, and his view remains with us today. Courage is exceptionally important because it aids a person in actually following through with all of the other moral virtues. The most important of these, Plato told us in his classic, *The Republic*, is justice or being fair to all. If we do not have fairness, we have no basis whatsoever for a well-functioning society. Courage helps us to follow laws, to accord respect to others in the family, and to demonstrate fair play at work and in all of our other social communities.

Courage is needed to forgive. Sometimes, as you know, it is difficult to start the process of having mercy on those who have been unfair to us. Courage helps us to start. Sometimes it is difficult to continue on the forgiveness journey because it is a struggle to keep going. Courage helps us here.

Courage does not involve moving forward in the absence of fear or discouragement. Instead, courage makes it possible for us to press forward when we do not feel our best. We go ahead with some fear, some discomfort, and even some lack of confidence that we can accomplish our goal.

So now to the next exercise: Think about one time in your life when you had to summon your courage to accomplish something and did so successfully. Just take a moment to let that image sink deeply into you. What is important about that image is that it actually happened to you. You went ahead, with courage, when you were not sure you could manage.

Now reflect on this truth you have just recognized. Try this wording to get started: "I have shown courage in the past. I am capable of showing courage now and in the future. I will use courage to get through this process of forgiving the one who hurt me." You can start by making the commitment to forgive, or to start again if you have tried without much success.

As an addition to this exercise, now combine humility and courage inside of you and consider bringing both of these moral virtues with you as you forgive. These two virtues are a strong combination that assures balance. Humility, by itself, can become imbalanced and make you prone to placing yourself lower than the one who hurt you. Courage, by itself, can likewise become imbalanced and make you prone to placing yourself higher than the one who hurt you. Courage, without humility, is prone toward power seeking and domination. With humility, courage will help you to keep going respectfully, without the urge to dominate. So as you courageously make this decision to go ahead with the forgiveness process, try to appropriate humility by seeing the one who injured you as your human equal. This perspective may help you to open and go through the door of forgiveness with less fear and more confidence.

Reminder 49:

The combination of humility and courage helps you to avoid excessive self-criticism and excessive criticism of others.

Exercise #8: A Little at a Time

Ours is a hurry-up world. We eat our meals fast, listen to part of a song before switching to another, read the first one-third of a book and leave it. We expect instant coffee, instant oatmeal, and instant results. This is not the way we should be approaching the forgiveness journey. We need to take it slowly.

Some of the major issues we have discussed so far on this forgiveness journey are listed in the following material. Your task is to determine on which of the particular issues you need to spend more time.

• Are you convinced that forgiveness matters for you? If so, how does it matter? And how convinced are you about this? Take some time reflecting on this as a way to gain confidence.

• How angry are you with the person you have in mind right now? If you are very angry, then you need to slow down the journey and work in a repeated way with some of the exercises for Key 3 as you confront the inner struggle and give yourself a chance to see the depth of the wound. The deeper the wound, the more time you will need.

• Have you begun to see the one who hurt you as a child growing up and incurring his or her own wounds? You may need more time here to think about the person in his or her childhood context and the challenges faced.

• How much time have you given to imagining this person as an adolescent and as an adult? Reviewing these perspectives can help you form a truer picture of this person, a picture that does not easily fade. Sometimes, although we can see that he or she is wounded, we just set aside that new recognition as we continue the inner dialogue about how awful this person is. Have you gone back to such an inner dialogue? If so, spend more time with Key 4.

• What about finding meaning in your suffering? Are you convinced that there is meaning? Have you spent enough time on the exercises to have found the true meaning or meanings for your particular circumstance? If not, spend more time with Key 5. Take your time. Do not rush the healing.

Exercise #9: Practice Patience

Do you find that you get annoyed with yourself for not making faster progress in forgiving? This is an inner judgment that can lead to anger at yourself. You certainly do not need another emotional wound, especially one that is self-inflicted. So use this exercise to help you develop the virtue of patience as you proceed. There are three parts to it.

First, use one potentially irritating situation with another person and practice patience toward that person. Intentionally try to be slow to anger; be slow to respond with words that could hurt the other, even if only a little. Of course, do not ignore injustices that need correction, but in those other situations, in which another is having a hard day, the task is patience.

Second, for today, be aware of any activity that is not going well for you. Check your inner world to see how you are talking to yourself about it and then say something like this to yourself: "I will be patient with myself. I will not be harsh with myself over this. The harshness only adds to my wounds, and I have enough of those." What you learned about being patient with another should now be applied to yourself.

Third, now do the same for the forgiveness journey. Say something like this to yourself: "This journey will take some time. I will not rush it, and I will practice the virtue of patience with myself as I proceed." Try to be aware each time you begin losing patience with yourself and repeat the statement, "I already have a lot of inner wounds. I will be patient with myself so that I do not add to those wounds."

Exercise #10: The Strategic Use of Time

For anything that is important to you, doesn't it seem to go better if you set aside a particular time on particular days to get that job accomplished? For example, we all know that if we want to work out regularly at a gym, it is best if we have set times and stick with those. It is the same with homework or other career tasks. And it is the same with the forgiveness journey.

For this exercise think through your weekly schedule with the plans you have for each day. When will you have time to add a slot for the practice of forgiveness into any given day? How much time do you want to spend on forgiveness on each of these days? I recommend that you write out the schedule and even set reminders on your computer or phone to be sure that you do the forgiveness work when you have the time to do so.

Even here you will have to practice gentleness toward yourself. Life is not easy, as we know, and so some of the time you will not be able to turn to forgiveness when it is scheduled. That is okay, as long as it does not become a habit and you let the forgiveness journey fade from your thoughts and actions.

Exercise #11: Be Aware of and Practice Applying a Strong Will

Lawrence was aware that he never quite finished whatever he started. One task was to refinish the doors to the three bedrooms in his and his partner's home. He finished one, but the others were left unattended. He took an online course on word processing and only completed one-third of the lessons. His attention span was short and his will to correct that was weak.

When his partner, Elizabeth, developed cancer, they both attended the lengthy set of treatments for her. Because she had some difficulty with mobility, they were driven to the clinic in a van. The driver was Christopher. He, too, had experienced considerable life challenges because of a serious car accident in which he had almost died. He has recovered to the fullest extent possible, but his speech was a bit slurred, he walked with a noticeable limp, and he experienced constant pain. He acted as a coach for Elizabeth and Christopher: "I want you to know that during this treatment process," he began, "you will want to give up. In fact, I know from experience that you will get to a point and you will say, 'I just can't go on any more.' I am here to tell you that you can and you will go on. When you get to that point, please remember me. You will summon the inner strength. So, when you get to that point, you must go on. You have no other choice."

Christopher was right. It did get to a point where both Elizabeth and Lawrence felt that they could not go on. Both were exhausted by the cancer treatments, and Lawrence's already weak will was showing itself. Yet he did not forget Christopher's counsel to them, and he summoned the will to move forward no matter what. He actually ended up giving great support to Elizabeth in her development of a strong will, and she did complete the treatment process with good results so far. The strong will led to success. Christopher's words proved to be highly important during this process.

Now it's your turn. For this first of two exercises here, listen to Christopher's words, now directed to you: "I want you to know that at some point in this forgiveness process you will want to give up. I am here to tell you that your inner resolve is much, much stronger than you even realize. Give your strong will a chance to shine. You can and will move forward toward healing."

For the second exercise, consider deliberately practicing and deepening your strong will in areas that are unrelated to forgiveness. Like Lawrence, you have tasks to do around the home. Make a list of three necessary tasks that need to be accomplished this week. Write them down and figure out which days are best to start and then to complete each one. Work on accomplishing what you are now committing to do as written out. Check back with the list from time to time to see how your strong will is developing as you finish these tasks. The point, of course, is now for you to apply this strong will to your forgiveness tasks.

A strong will leads to new behaviors of perseverance, a theme we discussed in Key 2. Start with the inner resolve of developing a strong will and then let that flow out to how you do the actual work of forgiving. Bring along those whom you have identified in Exercise #4 as supports for you as you proceed.

Reminder 50:

Having a strong will helps you to continue to forgive even when you are tired and want to walk away.

Exercise #12: Know and Practice Bearing the Pain

When you suffer from another's injustice, if you quietly endure that suffering, you are giving a gift to those around you by not passing on anger, frustration, or even hatred to them. Too often, people tend to displace their own frustrations and angers onto unsuspecting others. These others, then, end up inheriting the original person's internal

wounds because this person refused to bear the pain him-
or herself.

I am not saying here that it is good to shoulder psychological depression or unhealthy anger by being silent and
keeping it all in. On the contrary, here is the point: What
happened to you is now a reality. It did happen and you
cannot change that. You have inherited a certain amount of
pain from another person. What will you now do with that
pain? Will you try to toss it onto someone else in the hope
that it somehow leaves you? Or will you accept that this
hurtful event in fact happened and you will not now pass
the pain down the line to others? Consider taking this perspective in bearing the pain and if it is helpful return to
these ideas over the next week and whenever you feel
weakened, not wanting to go on with forgiveness:

> "If I can shoulder this pain now, I will not be passing it on to
> other people, even innocent people who never had any-
> thing at all to do with the original offense. My anger could
> be transferred to innocent people and they, in turn, could
> pass on this anger to someone else, who passes it to some-
> one else, and down the generations my anger goes. Do I
> want that? Do I want my anger to live on as it is transferred
> for many years to come? I can prevent this from happening
> as I decide, today, to bear the pain that came my way. I will
> not call what happened to me 'good.' It was not. But I will
> do my best to shoulder it, and, paradoxically, that pain is
> likely to start lifting from my shoulders as I accept it now.
> This pain is not forever and my bearing the pain may help
> reduce it faster."

Reminder 51:

As you bear the pain of what happened to you, you may be
protecting others and future generations from your anger.

Exercise #13: The Forgiveness Heroes Are Your Models

Sometimes it helps to summon your courage when you see and identify with those who have heroically forgiven, despite great odds against them. For this exercise, I recommend that you come alongside the forgiveness heroes whom you met as we explored Key 1. Reread their stories and use the narratives to gather your strength for your own journey. Write at least a sentence about each story that especially moves you and gives you motivation to keep persevering in forgiving. Each of the heroes overcame by forgiving. You can as well. Let their success inspire you to press on toward the goal of emotional relief and perhaps, for some of you, a renewed relationship as you give forgiveness and the other seeks and receives your forgiveness. Reunion is possible.

Here is one more instance of a forgiveness hero, someone who did not make the headlines. You already met Josiah in Key 5. He is a physical education teacher at the local high school and the boys' varsity basketball coach. He thought of quitting his job and taking disability payments after suffering paraplegia, but he decided to keep working to regain the strength to do his job. He started by trying to forgive the man who ran into his car.

He went to a lawyer and tried to arrange for a face-to-face meeting with the man, but he refused. So without even having seen his face, Josiah started on a full year's journey of forgiving him for what he had done. Josiah saw him as probably feeling intense guilt because of the car crash and the injury it caused and perhaps even feeling deep embarrassment, as suggested by his refusal to meet. Josiah reasoned that this man's inner torment of guilt might be even worse than his own disabling injuries. He was able to forgive this man and to gain an inner peace without distorting the incident in any way.

About a year and a half after the accident, the man, Adam, finally agreed to meet with Josiah with two lawyers present. At the meeting, Josiah learned that Adam had recently lost his son to cancer. In his grief, he was self-medicating and not paying attention, and he admitted that he should not have been driving at the time. Josiah stated that he had forgiven him and it helped Adam to apologize sincerely. In a way, this meeting seemed to give both of them a fresh start in life.

Josiah retained his jobs as physical education instructor and basketball coach, providing instruction from his wheelchair. At first he felt very awkward being in this kind of a profession while in a wheelchair, but whenever he heard any negative comments, he immediately began to forgive the speaker for a lack of understanding and compassion. And he thrived, despite the challenges.

Exercise #14: Forgiving for the Other More Than for the Self

This exercise taps into another paradox of forgiveness. We seem to do better when we step outside of our own specific interest and reach out to another in mercy, even if this does not seem entirely reasonable to do at the present time. As we give, it is we, the givers, who start to feel better. That is the paradox of this particular exercise. In this exercise, say to yourself—but only if you are ready: "I am doing the forgiving for the one who hurt me. This person is a wounded person, and I am doing what I can for [name]. Perhaps my forgiving will get his [her] attention. Perhaps this will be the beginning of change in him [her]." Try to say this three times a day until the idea is a part of you.

Such a perspective takes time and therefore requires your own inner gentleness, strong will, and perseverance. If this particular exercise seems reasonable to you, then do not give up. If you can, then please persevere in this perspective because it is one of the deepest experiences of what it means to forgive.

Exercise #15: Revise Your Perspectives on Power and Love if Necessary

Let's consider, once again, the information from Key 2 to gain some insight into how you have been talking with yourself about the challenging times when you find it hard to forgive. If you are clinging to the perspective of power, this stance is likely to get in the way of a satisfying forgiveness response. In this exercise examine some of the views of power and love to see on which side you are landing today.

> Power says, "I must hammer away at this process of forgiveness and achieve."
> Love says, "I'm imperfect and I have to respect the forgiveness process, even if it takes time."
>
> Power clings to resentment.
> Love wants to be done with the resentment.
>
> When power is not clinging to resentment, it wants no anger or inner disruption left at all.
> Love realizes that such anger can come back and is not unsettled by this.
>
> Power makes you feel inferior if you do not finish the forgiveness process.
> Love reminds you that it takes time to grow into a forgiveness response.
>
> Power encourages you not to forgive.
> Love considers forgiveness to be highly valuable.
>
> Power wants to get even.
> Love endures through knowing that you are both equal in your shared humanity.

Have you been looking at your forgiveness progress through the perspective of power or love? The forgiveness process does not

happen quickly; even if some anger remains after striving for forgiveness for a period of time, this only shows that you are human.
You have suffered enough without your demanding more from
yourself than you are able to give *right now*. Any progress toward
forgiveness is, in fact, progress. Allow yourself to feel encouraged.

Exercise #16: Finding Meaning in Sacrifice

When you sacrifice for others, you are doing a lot more
than acting in service to them. They may be bleeding emotionally inside, and you then bleed inside to help them
stop bleeding inside. For example, Brian's mother, Yolanda,
was overly controlling toward him and his partner, Simone.
Instead of distancing himself from Yolanda, he spent time
gently giving her examples of her not letting him, in her
own mind, develop independence in adulthood. This took
energy, a checking of his anger so it did not spill out to her,
and some suffering on his part to help her to understand.

Of course, we have to exercise temperance here, too.
Sacrifice does not mean that you do damage to yourself.
The paradox is that as you sacrifice for others, *you* experi-
ence emotional healing.

Dr. Frankl, in his book, *Man's Search for Meaning*, provides a remarkable case study of the kind of meaning one
can find in sacrificing for others. His example is not in the
context of forgiveness. I relate it to you so that you can see
how sacrifice works and becomes an aid to the one who is
doing the sacrificing. An elderly physician came to see Dr.
Frankl because of the loss of his wife two years earlier. Dr.
Frankl saw that he was psychologically depressed. His
question to the physician was this: "What would have happened to your wife if you were the one to go first?" With
that question a bigger picture opened for the physician.
Had he gone first, then it would have been his beloved
wife who would be visiting Dr. Frankl for her depression. By
her going first, she was spared years of grief. The physician

then understood that he could willingly take on the suffering on behalf of his wife.

Dr. Frankl then gives the reader an insight that is worth remembering: Sacrifice changes as soon as it is linked to a sound meaning that underlies it. The physician now had a meaning for going on, and his willing acceptance of outliving his wife was a sign that he loved her and wanted her safe.

Consider Lea's example. She had been married to Drake for five years. In that time, Drake had struggled greatly in his emotional life. After his mother died, he turned to both drink and gambling, stealing from their joint savings account and from her mother and father. Lea had tried for three years to get Drake to enter therapy with her. Finally, given Drake's unrelenting refusal, the therapist had recommended divorce. Lea, however, looked at the big picture for Drake. He had married her and moved to the part of the United States where she lived, leaving his family on the West Coast. She saw that if she divorced him, he would have no one as a support.

She saw glimmers of hope in him. He was beginning, in a small way, to see that his drinking, gambling, and stealing were wrong and hurtful. He was not sure how to stop. Although Lea had no guarantees, she was willing to sacrifice her happiness now for the possibility of a renewed relationship.

The therapist challenged her perspective, telling her that Drake was showing a cyclical pattern of abuse, then repentance, followed by abuse once again. The therapist believed that the pattern was not going to change.

Lea, instead, decided to work with Drake on forgiving his mother for her constant criticism of him when he was growing up. His mother rarely showed her approval (let alone praise) of him during his growing-up years, and as a result, he felt inadequate as a person. He detested himself, actually. Once Lea was able to help him forgive his mother, they turned to his own self-hatred. He worked on forgiving himself for all of the abuse that he threw onto others as a direct result of the abuse he had suffered in childhood.

Eventually—it took over a year—Drake's hatred diminished, his drinking became more temperate, and he stopped gambling altogether. Lea had saved Drake's life and their relationship. Her sacrificial response was part of forgiving Drake and standing with him as they both healed their wounded hearts. Of course, not all relationships like Drake and Lea's have such a happy ending, particularly if one or both refuse to change. In this case, both spouses needed to change. Drake had to decrease his hatred toward his mother and himself, and Lea had to reduce her resentment toward Drake. Without the sacrificial attitude that Dr. Frankl had found therapeutic when he examined meaning in his own life, Lea's path in life would have been different. I can hear some saying, "You've got that right. She would have been finished with the pain long before if she had dumped him." Yet that is not the way Lea now sees it. She sees that she made a profoundly difficult relationship work. She sees that she overcame. And she knows that she played a part in this transformation. All of this adds meaning to her life and happiness within.

Now to the exercise, which has two parts:

1. Can you see how a sacrificial attitude, within reason, could aid you in forgiving and in overcoming resentment? I say *within reason* because you do not want to overdo this either. If a person refuses to hear what you have to say, or refuses to accept your sacrificial gestures and begins to use you, then it is time to reexamine the approach. None of these approaches is foolproof. If you see benefit in the sacrificial attitude and related behaviors, then what is your particular plan? Write it down and consider these questions as well: What will you do that is hard for you to do in ser-

vice to the other? How long will you give this undertaking? Do you see even a glimmer of evidence, as Lea did in Drake, that the other is open to even small change? Be sure to monitor your coping level during this exercise so that the sacrifice does not lead to an even greater resentment. If that begins to happen over a period of time, then it is time to reevaluate this particular approach in your case. If, on the other hand, it seems to be working, then stay at it as long as you can and as long as the other is willing to work with you in changing behaviors.

2. In this part of the exercise, reflect on the possibility that without your forgiveness, that person may never learn to live well. You may be playing a part in helping him or her grow deeply as a person. How might that be? He or she is being given a chance to see what genuine love is and to see it in action. Your sacrificial approach may even be playing a part in the very survival of this person. Of course, you do not want to go so far with this sacrifice that you do damage to yourself. Instead, the point here is that as you give of yourself, *within reason*, this giving might prove to be emotionally healing for *you*. When you are ready, write down your answer to the question of how you may be aiding the other's healing.

Reminder 52:

Sacrifice is a *reaching out* to the other, within reason, even when it is uncomfortable to do so.

Exercise #17: Practice on an Easier Case

If you have read to this point in the book and are still having a hard time forgiving a particular person, perhaps it is time to take a step back and start to forgive a different person. Let's return to the "practice person" I mentioned earlier in the book. The point here is to develop your forgiveness fitness without going to the heavy weights first.

I recommend that you put aside, for now, the work you have been doing and turn instead to this practice person. Remain on the forgiveness journey until you experience internal relief and can truly say, "I forgive this person." Remember that you need not forgive perfectly, and thus you may have some anger left over, but if you are in control of that anger, then you have completed the forgiveness journey for now. Then turn back to the one whom you find it hard to forgive and go through the same process—which is now more familiar to you.

Exercise #18: Start with Another Person Who Might Be Even Harder to Forgive

When we were on Key 4, I mentioned that sometimes we have to set aside our forgiveness of one person because there is yet someone else who is getting in the way of forgiving the one we are currently considering. And so we revisit that now, which may seem a bit odd, given that I just asked you to forgive someone who is easier to forgive.

I actually am not contradicting myself. I do recommend, when you find forgiving to be hard, to step back and try forgiving someone who is easier to forgive. Once you have gained confidence this way, it may be time to examine the issue of whether or not there is someone who needs to be forgiven before you start on the one you currently find hard to forgive. Here is an example.

Consider Lea and Drake's relationship. If Drake starts to forgive himself first, he is likely to find that images of his mother come popping into his mind as he tries to self-forgive. Why? Because his difficult relationship with his mother caused great inner pain, he self-medicated to temporarily block that pain. So whenever he thinks back to incidents in which he drank to excess, there will be his mother in his mind, scolding him, withdrawing love from him, and making him feel small. With this kind of image in his mind and heart, how easy will it be for him to offer compassion toward himself when he is feeling an inner rage, this time directed at his mother?

His forgiveness journey toward himself will be more effective if he can first reduce the rage he has toward his mother. Then, with that emotion quieted at least to a significant degree, he can start to forgive himself without that added rage getting in the way.

You, too, might have started on the forgiveness path with someone and yet whenever you think of that person, you begin to think of another person who is making you so angry that you cannot concentrate on the forgiveness work. If this is the case for you, then it's essential to identify who this other person is. How much anger do you have? Do you think that your forgiving this person first might free you to do the forgiveness work with the one you initially identified as appropriate for your forgiveness?

If the answer is *yes* to the previous question, then perhaps it is time to gently set aside your original plan, forgive this new person, and then go back to the other. You may find that your forgiveness progresses better.

Exercise #19: Turning Your Forgiveness Efforts Over to a Higher Power

As you may know, in the Alcoholics Anonymous program (and other related self-help programs), people are encouraged to turn over their cravings, temptations, and their healing to a "higher power." This more generic term *higher power* is meant to be broad enough to encompass many people's beliefs.

This same procedure can be used when a person is feeling powerless over the ability to forgive. In 1986 the psychiatrist Richard Fitzgibbons published an article in an American Psychological Association journal recommending this very process for particularly difficult cases of forgiveness. When people cannot seem to shed their anger using psychological approaches to healing, this "higher power" way can prove to be beneficial.

If you have a belief system that transcends the physical world, are you willing to turn over your resentment to the higher power (you should use the name that is appropriate for you)? Are you willing to surrender your feelings and rest in the faith that you will be assisted on the journey? This is not to suggest that you passively leave all of your own work there. When you need time to rest and gain strength, you should consider a total surrender and then do the work you need to do in cooperation with this higher power when you are feeling more refreshed.

Exercise #20: When the Injustice Is Incomprehensible

Sometimes the injustice is so cruel and cuts so deeply into us that we are unable to make any sense of what happened. And when people are confronted by such cruel acts, they are likely to feel confused and frightened. They start to wonder what this world is all about. They question the motives of all people. They question the existence of the "higher power" and can turn away from their faith. Confronting the problem of incomprehensible cruelty in this world—after the injustice has occurred—can do more to hurt a person than the original offense can. I say this because confronting this kind of severe injustice can lead to very pessimistic views of humanity, of the motivations of friends, and the possibility of ever being happy in a relationship.

An answer that I like to give when a person is overcome by the question of immense cruelty in the world is this: We all have free will. One person deciding to act badly does not mean that all people will choose to operate in a similar, bad way. Good in the form of justice does exist in this world, and so does free will. We have to be careful in thinking that all is beyond justice and order and there is no true good in the world. Such an outlook can quickly lead to despair.

Now to the exercise: Has another's cruelty destroyed (at least for now) your belief that people can be good? Has the incomprehensible injustice destroyed (at least for now) your belief in a higher power? In the vast majority of religions the higher power is seen as allowing the individual expression of free will out of respect for each person's individuality, so poor choices are deemed inevitable in a world such as ours. Are you aware of this view or have you turned your back on the transcendent altogether? If so, has this turning away from a source beyond yourself been good for your well-being or not? It is important to ask the hard questions about cruelty in this world, the higher power, your response to both, and your difficult path of forgiveness. Is it possible that your worldview, including what you believe incomprehensible injustice is and how it operates in this world, could be making you even angrier than the original offense against you?

Reminder 53:

If you have believed in a higher power, do not turn against the higher power because someone turned against you.

Questions Regarding When Forgiveness Is Hard

Question 1

"I have done the exercises here, but I'm still not sure that I will be able to forgive the one who hurt me because I'm still angry. How do I proceed now?"

When examining Key 3, I made the point that one of your wounds may be a lack of confidence in your own ability to heal emotionally. I bring this up because this issue may still be getting in your way as you travel the forgiveness path. Examine this issue of self-confidence and if it is lacking in you, go to Exercise #17 and begin doing the forgiveness work with someone who is easier to forgive. As you gain some success with this, you will be more prepared to advance to forgiving those who are particularly difficult to offer such mercy.

Question 2

"I have been working on forgiveness for months now and I still have anger. I think that this anger is a sign that I am not forgiving. Can you help me?"

This question differs from the preceding question in this way: In the first question the person was struggling with self-confidence; in this question the person is struggling with left-over anger. So now the question back to him or her is this: How much anger do you have? Is it controlling you? If not, and if you have felt your anger lessen, then you are heading in the right direction.

We have to be careful not to expect perfection on this forgiveness journey. Yes, it is the case that for some people the anger goes away completely and rarely, if ever, returns. For others, the anger goes up and down. The important point is to assess how intense the anger gets when it returns. If it is moderate (when it used to be severe) and if it lasts for a shorter time, then be gentle with yourself in this area. The late Lewis Smedes gave good advice in his book *Forgive and Forget* when he emphasized that you know you are forgiving when you wish the person well. Do you have some residual anger and yet wish the person well? Then you are forgiving and you need to give yourself credit for this.

Toward Your Future When Forgiveness Is Hard

I think that you will find forgiveness to be a familiar friend the more you persevere and practice it . . . again and again. Forgiveness is not a skill. It is a moral virtue with certain keys to assist you as you grow in this virtue. And yet there is a certain skill component to it. As you practice forgiveness, the mind of forgiveness gets sharper, you turn more readily toward finding a good and true meaning in your suffering, and you even grow to recognize what the suffering is like so that it is not a scary mystery any more. As you practice forgiveness, you grow in confidence as a forgiver. And then you realize that even the hard cases of forgiveness, although never easy, can be confronted more quickly with deeper and more satisfying results as you become a forgiving person.

We turn now to another key, one that many consider part of "when it's hard to forgive." That key is self-forgiveness.

LEARN TO FORGIVE YOURSELF

The one who hurt you . . .
  passed his or her unhappiness to you
  leaving a mess for you to clean up now in your heart.
Will you . . .
  pass this unhappiness now to others
  so that they can clean up a mess?
Or will you . . .
  forgive and stop the passing on of unhappiness and messes?
Oh . . . and the one who hurt you is yourself.

For some reason, the lock that opens with Key 7 is a little harder to turn than were the other locks on the other six doors. Perhaps it is because most of us tend to be harder on ourselves than we are on others. The focus in the room which this key opens is . . . you. It is not entirely on you, as you will see, but a lot of the material here centers on you and your hurting yourself as you broke your own standards of right and wrong. Do not feel isolated and alone in that thought. All of us on the planet have done so; we have *all* broken our own standards. Let's look into the lives of two such people, Pedro and Jennifer, as we do the work of self-forgiveness.

Pedro is 47 years old, owns a landscape business, and is tormented inside. He is having regrets about how he interacted with his now-deceased father. He once told his father that he was worthless and walked out of the house. When Pedro returned, his father would not look at him. Now that his father is deceased,

Pedro cannot ask directly for forgiveness. He feels trapped with the immature choice he made when he was younger.

His torment is increased now that his two children are grown and gone from the home. He regrets not having spent enough time with them when they were younger. He was so busy building his business that he would come home late and tired, unable to give them the attention that growing children need. He feels now that he never bonded appropriately with them, and the accuracy of his view is confirmed by the fact that they seldom visit. There is a distance between them that he sees as hopeless to cross.

Pedro cannot take back the words he spoke to his father. He cannot take back the stealing of time (as he calls it) from his children. He says that he is stuck. He dislikes himself for the regrets he carries every day.

Pedro is not as hopeless as he thinks. There is hope for a renewed relationship with the children and a greater self-acceptance if he can do the work of self-forgiveness.

Jennifer, at age 22, took a position as an office assistant. The pay was not quite enough for a living wage because she was living in a large, expensive city. As the keeper of the financial books, she started to skim small amounts of money each week and over a period of two years, she accumulated several thousand dollars, all stolen from the company.

She now is married with a child and is profoundly disappointed with herself for her immature behavior from years ago. While the company in no way was devastated by the skimming, it was clear to Jennifer that this was not her money to take. She was mortified to tell her husband and she did not want to mention anything to the owners of the company, even though she had not worked for them for the past five years, just in case she needed to go back to work. Getting a letter of recommendation would be impossible. She hated herself and lived with intense guilt while trying to be a good wife and mother. And it was increasingly difficult for her because of the guilt that seemed to have no solution. As a religious person, she had asked God to forgive her and although she felt helped by this, she still could not rid herself of the shame, especially because she never gave back the money. She felt that she needed to do something or she would burst, in an emotional sense. She is finally considering forgiving herself for stealing.

You should know that this theme—self-forgiveness—is controversial in the psychological literature. Our first task, then, is for you to see this controversy and my response to it. You can then decide whether or not self-forgiveness is for you. If it is, then you can proceed to a series of exercises to help you forgive yourself for your unjust behaviors.

The Controversy Surrounding Self-Forgiveness

Self-forgiveness is controversial primarily because of a journal article written by a respected colleague, Paul Vitz, and his coauthor, Jennifer Meade, in the *Journal of Religion and Health* in 2011.[10] In that article, the authors criticize self-forgiveness in at least five ways. We will be considering each of these here, plus a final sixth issue. If you are worried that there is no such thing as self-forgiveness or that it is an inappropriate way to forgive, then I urge you to read these next six sections. They will get quite philosophical because my response requires that if I will be clear. Otherwise, if you already are convinced that self-forgiveness is reasonable and appropriate when you break your own moral standards, then please move ahead to the section entitled, "So, Then, What Is Self-Forgiveness?" (p.181).

Let's consider each of the criticisms of self-forgiveness now.

For Religious People, There Are No Directives to Self-Forgive

Vitz and Meade make the point that because there are no written documents from ancient times that encourage people to forgive

---

[10] Vitz, P. C., & Meade, J. (2011). Self-forgiveness in psychology and psychotherapy: A critique. *Journal of Religion and Health, 50,* 248–259. doi: 10.1007/s10943-010-9343-x

themselves, it is unimportant or improper to do so. Yet it seems to me that there *are* directives for self-forgiveness. For example, in the Hebrew Bible, particularly the Book of Leviticus, people are encouraged to love their neighbors as they love themselves. This directive is reiterated in the Christian New Testment, particularly in the Gospels of Matthew and Mark. The implicit assumption in this directive is that we *do* love ourselves—it's assumed—and that this self-love should serve as the basis of extending an equally loving attitude toward our neighbors. So an important point is that these teachings assume we love ourselves. What is forgiveness when offered to other people? It is to love those who have offended you. If you have offended yourself, is it not then appropriate to love yourself again when you are not feeling such love? The answer seems to be yes. We are to love ourselves, and when we have deeply offended ourselves, we are to work our way back to self-love, which in this case requires engaging in self-forgiveness.

Self-Forgiveness "Splits" the Person into a Good Self and a Bad Self

Vitz and Meade make the challenging claim that when a person self-forgives, he or she sees a good self (who forgives) and a bad self (who committed the bad deeds). This psychological splitting of the self into two, the good and the bad, is confusing for the self-forgiver, they contend, and therefore psychologically unhealthy.

Consider these questions in response: Can we make the important distinction between *who* you are as a person and *what you do* in a behavioral sense as a person? Are we not all prone to errors and to regrettable behavior from time to time? When we engage in regrettable acts, do we say that this is our "bad self" operating or do we more accurately say that we *behaved* badly? Can you see the very large difference between condemning your entire being—yourself as a person—and being disappointed in *what you do*? It seems to me that Vitz and Meade are making an important point, not about self-forgiveness itself, but rather about how it can be *distorted*. Instead of saying, "I am a bad/worthless/stupid person," when we prepare to forgive ourselves, instead we should be saying, "I did something bad, but I am still a person of inherent worth in spite of my struggles and imperfections." After all, when we forgive other people, we do not see them as bad *people* but as having *done a bad thing*. Our task is to reawaken in ourselves, as forgivers of others, that sense of inherent worth in the offending person.

Is it not the same in self-forgiveness? Can't we separate our very personhood from our behavior at a given time, rather than creating two separate selves? It seems to me that if people created two separate selves, a good one and a bad one, they would be engaging in a false kind of self-forgiveness and need to correct this. It is not the "fault" of self-forgiveness that a person misunderstands the concept and "splits" his or her view of him- or herself into good and bad selves. Neither is it the "fault" of self-forgiveness when a person fails to recognize his or her inherent worth because of "bad" behavior. The problem here of "splitting" resides in false psychological views of the self and so this criticism does not apply to those of us who wish to engage in self-forgiveness.

Embedded in Self-Forgiveness Is a Conflict of Interest between the Judging Self and the Self That Is Judged

Vitz and Meade make the excellent point that we should not be our own judge when we do wrong. For example, suppose someone is in court for auto theft. It would be outrageous if the court of law allowed that person to pass judgment on his or her own guilt or innocence. They conclude that to self-forgive is wrong because one is both a defendant (who did wrong) and a judge (letting oneself off the hook): a conflict of interest.

Yet does the forgiveness of other people ever take place in a court of law? Never. Yes, someone could be watching a court hearing and engage in forgiving, but it is never the judge who forgives because the judge must be impartial. If the judge even has the potential to need to forgive, this would mean that he or she were offended and therefore should not be presiding over this particular case. When we forgive other people (not the self), we are not presiding over (judging) the other as if we are to hand out a punishment or not. We instead are exercising a virtue of mercy by trying to love someone who did not love us, who was unfair to us. Cannot we do the same in self-forgiveness by refraining from placing the forgiving action in a court of law, which actually distorts the essence of what forgiveness is?

When we self-forgive, we are not releasing ourselves from self-punishment. Instead we are trying to love ourselves so that we can rid ourselves of self-hatred, which itself seems to be a kind of "splitting" of who we are (as someone deserving of both love and hatred). So in this case, self-forgiveness might actually play a part in reducing the psychological distortion of "splitting" and help the person to "live with" him- or herself in a more loving way.

In summary, we are not in a court of law when we self-forgive. We are doing our best to reestablish a love of self that has been lost because of our behavior.

Self-Forgiveness Can Distort
What Is a Fair Self-Reparation

This notion follows directly from the assertion that one cannot be one's own judge because one cannot see clearly to know what is a good reparation (which means, a good and just response to fix the problem) for the self. As we have seen, forgiveness itself, as one aspect of being merciful, is not about asking other people who have hurt us to make reparation to us. When we do this kind of asking, we have switched from exercising mercy and forgiveness to now exercising the virtue of justice. Thus, when we self-forgive, we do not ask the self for a kind of reparation or a fixing of what we did to the self.

Even if we did engage in asking ourselves for reparation, is this any different from the dangers of distorting what we ask for when we hold others accountable for repairing what they did to us? Whenever we have been hurt by other people, we have a tendency, out of anger, to exaggerate the kind and amount of reparation necessary to somehow fix what was done to us. We can seek others' counsel to help us ask for as fair a solution as possible. My point is that reparation is never a clear issue when we, ourselves, make the decision, especially when we are angry.

As a final point here, we are always engaging in self-evaluating our imperfections. For example, suppose you have a tendency to eat too much or to exercise too little or to be impatient with others. Do you stop short of self-improvement efforts because you cannot know exactly how imperfect you are or exactly what to do for improvement? Don't you go ahead anyway? Self-forgiveness also involves a quest toward self-improvement in that we have failed to love ourselves as we should, even in the face of disappointing behavior, and we do our best to (1) see that we have offended ourselves, (2) recognize the need to welcome ourselves back to true humanity rather than engaging in self-loathing, and (3) start the process of loving ourselves again as the way back to that sense of full humanity.

Self-Forgiveness Is an Extreme Emphasis on Self, Which Can Produce Narcissism

Suppose you had an accident in which your leg was deeply cut, requiring stitches. Would it be "extreme" of you to focus on that cut, put energy into going to the emergency room, and taking time and effort to heal the wound? Of course not. In fact, it would be psychologically and physically healthy to deal with this physical wound.

When another person has been cruel to you, is it extreme if you focus on the process of forgiving that person, putting time and energy into forgiveness that can heal your emotions? Of course not. It is a healthy response.

And yet, even these quests for healing one's leg and one's damaged emotions from others' unjust actions can be distorted to such a point that your actions actually become unhealthy. For example, suppose in the cleaning and bandaging of your wounded leg, you spent 10 hours a day on what should take 15 minutes. What if you ignore your family when trying to forgive others, hide in your room, and compulsively do the work of forgiveness? These kinds of behaviors are out of balance relative to a healthy way to go about physical and emotional healing.

Is it not the same with self-forgiveness? We need not spend 10 hours a day on it or hide in our room as we ignore family and focus on nothing but the self. This is not the "fault" of self-forgiveness but instead of a distortion of it. Again, Vitz and Meade provide a useful service to us with the message: Do not overdo this.

Self-forgiveness can be done in proper perspective, with the demands and needs of a full life in view. It need not lead to narcissistic self-pursuits any more than attending to a wounded leg or to emotions wounded by others' unfair actions. Cannot individuals engage in the virtue of forgiveness by focusing it on this person, then that person, then the self with success, and not in a way that "splits" their personalities or that lets them off the justice hook or compels them to engage in an obsessive self-focus?

Why Not Just Engage in Self-Acceptance Rather Than the Distorting Process of Self-Forgiveness?

In the final analysis, Vitz and Meade call for an entirely different approach: that of self-acceptance rather than self-forgiveness. In my opinion, might such a move create the exact same problems (with one exception) that the authors see in their views of self-forgiveness? After all, for the religious person, there is no call for explicit self-acceptance in ancient scriptures any more than there is for explicit self-forgiveness. Cannot we "split" ourselves into the unaccepted part and the accepted part? Won't we still need to repair what we damaged in the self when we engage in self-acceptance? Is not this self-reparation just as prone to distortion as is the reparation when we self-forgive? Might the quest for self-acceptance lead to an extreme focus on the self, especially if we are having a hard time accepting ourselves?

The one exception is the issue of a conflict of interest. Because one is not being a judge when self-accepting, then one avoids the conflict of interest. Yet, as I pointed out above, one is not being a judge when engaging in self-forgiveness either.

As a final point about self-acceptance, it seems to me that to engage in self-acceptance might be very difficult to do, even harder than self-forgiveness, because there are no carefully worked-out psychological processes for acceptance as there are for forgiveness. Can you imagine how difficult it would be if someone asked a rape victim to accept what the other had done to her? Why should it be different when it is the self who has offended? I think we need stronger medicine than acceptance when we shock ourselves by breaking our own moral standards—and forgiveness is that strong medicine. This is why I am concerned when the advice is to reject self-forgiveness. I would reject it if the criticisms against it were so strong as to make the case that it is dangerous, inappropriate, or an illusion. As you can see from my rebuttal to the criticisms of self-forgiveness, I do not see it as any of these things.

Reminder 54:

The warnings that self-forgiveness is either inappropriate or psychologically dangerous seem to focus more on false forms of it than on self-forgiveness itself.

Why Not Engage in a Temperate Form of Self-Love Rather Than Calling This Self-Forgiveness?

Although Vitz and Meade did not bring up this question, it follows directly from their discussion and so we should examine it. It seems to me that a balanced (not narcissistic) form of self-love in the particular context of having deeply offended the self *is* self-forgiveness. After all, when we think of forgiving other people, we are trying to love them. We only call this forgiveness when it is *in the context of being treated badly by the person*. So when we try to love in the context of injustice and hurt, the word for this is *forgiveness*; when we try to love in the context of injustice and hurt from the self, the word for this is *self-forgiveness*.

So, Then, What Is Self-Forgiveness?

We have just seen that when you self-forgive, you are not engaging in something that is completely unaddressed in religious traditions. You are not "splitting" yourself into a good half and a bad half. You are not, in a symbolic sense, entering a court of law in which you become a judge over yourself. You are not engaging in self-reparation, although you are striving for self-improvement. You are not obsessing over yourself and lapsing into narcissism. And you are going beyond self-acceptance to deeper work.

When you self-forgive, you are practicing the virtue of mercy toward yourself. And this next point is very important: You continually extend virtues toward yourself, such as being fair to yourself (the virtue of justice), taking care of yourself (the virtues of kindness and wisdom), and being patient with yourself when you are learning new things in life. If you can practice all of these virtues toward yourself, why would anyone want to bar you from the most important of the moral virtues: loving yourself in the face of disappointment, disapproval, and in extreme cases, self-hatred?

When you self-forgive, you are struggling to love yourself when you are not feeling lovable because of your actions. You are offering to yourself what you offer to others who have hurt you: a sense that you have inherent worth, despite your actions; that you are more than your actions; that you can and should honor yourself as a person even if you are imperfect; and that you did wrong and need to correct that wrong *done to other people*. In self-forgiveness you never (as far as I have ever seen) offend yourself alone. You also offend others and so part of self-forgiveness is to deliberately engage in seeking forgiveness from those others and righting the wrongs (as best you can under the circumstances) that you did toward them. This is not *self*-reparation, as discussed by Vitz and Meade, but instead it is reparation *toward others*. Thus, we have two differences between forgiving others and forgiving the self. In the latter, you seek forgiveness from those hurt by your actions and you strive for justice toward them.

Reminder 55:

Self-forgiveness includes seeking forgiveness and making reparation toward those who were hurt by your actions (which also hurt you).

Exercise #1: Before Self-Forgiving: Are You Being Overly Harsh in Your Self-Judgment?

As Vitz and Meade pointed out, we can exaggerate and distort the process of self-forgiveness. One such distortion is to think that your misbehavior is much worse than it actually is. Consider an example. Once Mary's mother passed away, Mary was anxious for months over her thought that she had never done enough for her mother. Even though she took her mother into her own home for a year while she was dying, Mary was haunted by guilt. She even began to think of how she misbehaved as a child and therefore made her mother's parenting more difficult than it should have been.

Mary, in her grief, was looking for perfection in herself and, not finding it, condemned herself for mere human imperfections and not actual injustices. This kind of distorted thinking can happen when a loved one dies. The mourning process can reawaken our own injustices from years before. Those injustices are deep in the attic of our mind and only get dusted off as we reflect on the deceased person and how we could have done better for him or her. We want to take back some of the things we said or did. Sometimes, however, this kind of mourning ends up exaggerating our human imperfections, so self-forgiveness is not the prescription now. Instead, what is needed is a clearer assessment of those imperfections, the good intentions, and a conclusion that we are now overreacting.

Before you engage in self-forgiveness, you owe it to yourself to let yourself off the guilt hook if you are exaggerating your behavior, calling it very bad when it is merely normal human imperfection. This is not to minimize genuine injustices. At the same time, it is important to give yourself permission to let go of all those situations in which you are falsely accusing yourself. This letting go requires wisdom and courage. Are you willing to let go that which needs letting go? You should self-forgive only in the context of *genuine broken standards*.

For today, refrain from the audio recording in your head: "If only I had done more." You have done . . . a lot. It is time to set yourself free. Replace that recording in your head with this: "I am imperfect, but this does not mean that I am a bad person." Now take each step on the journey of self-forgiveness.

Exercise #2: Choose One Incident in Genuine Need of Self-Forgiveness

For this exercise, choose one legitimate event in which you broke your own standards and are feeling genuine guilt and disappointment with yourself. When did this event occur? What is it that you did to break your own standards of right and wrong? How badly are you feeling right now on a scale of 1–10? If you give this a 5 or higher, then you have chosen an event in need of self-forgiveness. Now for the next exercise.

Exercise #3: What Are Some Consequences of the Disappointing Behavior?

As you know from examining the process of forgiving others, when injustice happens, then certain consequences follow, such as anger, fatigue, preoccupation with the person for what happened, and even a change in how you see yourself. Either write in a journal or think through your story of these consequences as I ask you a series of questions.

1. How angry at yourself are you? Again, use the 1–10 scale for this rating. If you give your anger a rating of 9 or 10, then you have to decide if you might need some professional help. Sometimes we need assistance when our emotions are intense and long-lasting (say, more than two weeks).

When Pedro began to forgive himself for his actions toward his father and his children, he labeled his anger as an 8. He did not like himself. He knew that he had to practice patience as he worked through the issues, one at a time, regarding both father and children. Here it's important that you do the same. Focus on only one incident (from Exercise #2) so that you are not overwhelmed by this series of exercises and take breaks as you walk this path of self-forgiveness.

Do heed Vitz and Meade's counsel to beware of developing an excessive focus on yourself, which is not healthy. See this series of exercises as part of your overall life and not as your only task over the coming days and weeks. It may take months for you to conquer the anger that now is inside you. Again, have patience with yourself as you proceed.

2. Are you tired? Being angry at yourself can take up a lot of your energy. Jennifer began to realize that the energy she needed to care for her baby was being partially consumed by her anger toward herself. This is when she started to take seriously the idea of self-forgiveness. Are you less able to meet obligations because of the anger still present from your unacceptable behavior?

When dealing with anger, it is common to use distractions, to overdo, even to engage in sleep deprivation as a way to quiet the emotions. Check in with youself to see if the way in which you have been living your life has led to fatigue, so that you can break the pattern. What is one behavior in your life right now that needs changing so that you are less tired? Please write down some ideas about how to change the behavior that leads to the fatigue. This may become clearer as you advance in self-forgiveness.

3. How often do you think about this particular event or situation in which you broke your own standards? When there are problems to solve, sometimes people stay at the task until it is accomplished. I think it is a way of adapting to challenging situations so that they are met and accomplished. However, if you have offended yourself and have not found the path to self-forgiveness, you may be stuck in a cycle of thinking about, but not solving, your problem. It is as if the wheels of your car are caught in the mud with no way out. The harder you try, the deeper the tires go. When that happens in the context of self-offense, you may be spending a lot of low-quality time just ruminating about the issue—which, as you know, will not solve the problem. Try to become aware of your pattern of thinking about this event or situation. Are you obsessing over it? Do you have dreams about it? If so, what you did may be robbing you of your inner peace, further underscoring the need to change that pattern.

4. Finally, if you had to write a story about who you are as a person, what would you write? Do you see yourself as a failure? Do you see yourself as a little less worthy than the rest of humanity? When you break your own standards in a serious way, there is a danger of sliding into self-loathing. When this happens, you may not take good care of yourself. You might overeat or oversleep, give up exercising, or engage in other forms of self-subversion as a way to subconsciously punish yourself for what you did. Pedro began to smoke cigarettes, a habit he knew was not in his best interest. He was not concerned about the consequences of

such smoking because deep down, he felt that he was not
a very nice person. He did not like himself and so why go
out of his way to care for himself?

Are you engaging in even subtle forms of self-
punishment as a result of what you did? Write that story
now, if you are ready, about who you are as a person.
Include those themes of self-aversion and self-punishment,
if they exist for you. Then reflect on how you can re-write
the story to be more gentle with yourself. If you see self-
punishment in the story, take courage into your heart. It is
time to change this pattern of punishment through self-
forgiveness.

Exercise #4: Know What Self-Forgiveness Is and Is Not

It is . . . quiz time! Without looking back in this chapter,
write down or think through the definition of what self-
forgiveness is and what it is not. Try to be as accurate as
you can. The point of this exercise is for you to gain accurate knowledge of what you are about to do in self-
forgiveness. So, try to be as thorough as you can.

Now check back in this chapter to the section entitled
"So, Then, What Is Self-Forgiveness?" (p. 181). Are there
differences between your thoughts here and what is written
there? Did you leave out anything, such as the steps of
seeking forgiveness from others or striving for justice, as
best you can, when you were unjust? Are you convinced
that self-forgiveness is a good thing (as I think it is), or are
you hesitant, thinking it is inappropriate (as Vitz and Meade
say)? Proceed with the next set of exercises once you are
satisfied that you know what self-forgiveness is and therefore what is ahead on your path to emotional healing.

Exercise #5: Knowing More Deeply Who You Are
as a Person

What did you write about yourself in Exercise #3? Look for
all of the indications in that exercise in which you deny your

own inherent worth: that sense that you are special, unique, and irreplaceable. Each one of those statements is a lie and surely you do not want to continue lying to yourself about yourself.

Do you have inherent worth . . . right now? You are as special, unique, and irreplaceable as when you were a newborn infant. You are as special, unique, and irreplaceable as when you were a cute little toddler needing to give and receive love. You are as special, unique, and irreplaceable as when you were a teenager, trying to figure out what life is all about. No matter what has happened in your life, no matter what you have done to others, and no matter what you have done to yourself you are special . . . unique . . . and irreplaceable. If you do not believe this, try writing down for now one counter example showing your inherent worth. It exists and now I ask you to take the time to see this. After seeing and writing down this one manifestation of your inherent worth, I have one more exercise for you: Find a second example. It exists and you need to see it.

In the film *Forrest Gump*, the supposedly inept Forrest saves his lieutenant in Vietnam, but one aftermath of that saving is that Lieutenant Dan lost both of his legs in the attack on his unit. While he was engaging in self-loathing, lamenting that he no longer is who he was, Forrest looks at him and says with deep sincerity, "Y-you still Lieutenant Dan." The loss of his legs, of his current career, of his own positive judgment of himself did not detract even a little from the truth: He still is Lieutenant Dan. Are you still you? It is a big lie if you think you are not.

Reminder 56:

When you offend yourself, you might lose your own sense of inherent worth. It is time to reclaim the truth: You are a person of inherent worth.

Reflect on the following questions. If you disagree with any of them, try to counter the disagreement with a reasonable rebuttal. Do all people have this inherent worth even if they are unable to walk, as was the case with Lieutenant Dan? Do all people have inherent worth even if they lose all their money, or their loved ones, or their health? Do all people have inherent worth even if they let themselves down? If so, then you, too, possess this inherent worth even when you let yourself down.

Exercise #6: Having Compassion for Yourself

Have you ever helped someone who would not be able to help you in return, such as comforting a child or donating to a favorite charity or helping an elderly person lift a heavy object? What did you feel in your heart at that moment? Was it stoney cold or warm and loving? To have compassion is to *suffer with* the one who is suffering.

You are now the one suffering, so it's time to extend the compassion that you have felt for others to yourself. Soften your heart toward yourself—not because of anything you have done, good or bad. Soften your heart toward yourself simply and importantly because you are . . . *you.* You are someone who is suffering, and you can now be gentle with yourself as a hurting person. Get reacquainted with you. Here are some questions for your reflection in the journal: Are you more than your imperfections? Can you see yourself as wounded? When you reflect on your wounded-self, what does that do for your heart? Can you feel your heart being a little softer toward yourself? If so, this is the beginning of compassion.

When Pedro began to see that compassion toward himself was possible, he was able to forgive himself not only for his past behaviors but also for taking up cigarette smoking as a result of feeling great distress over his past choices. He realized that he was not loving himself by the cigarette smoking, but was only digging a deeper hole for himself in life.

It is time to welcome yourself back to the human condition—no matter what others say about you . . . no matter what you say about yourself . . . no matter what. Persevere in this quest for self-compassion, just as you have done for others at some time in your life. To persevere in this, I suggest that for at least one week you read your journal entry about your wounded-self and your softening heart as you realize just how wounded you are. Use this opportunity to develop and solidify this softer approach toward yourself.

Reminder 57:

See yourself as you are: as a person who is worthy of your time and respect and compassion, no matter what.

Exercise #7: Bear the Pain You Have Caused to Yourself and Others by Your Actions

In Key 6 you were introduced to Aaron, who deliberately decided to bear the pain when his wife was unfaithful. You engaged in a forgiveness exercise of bearing the pain that others have caused you by their injustice. It is now time to focus this kind of exercise on yourself because of what you have done. You already know what it feels like to bear the pain because it is not new to you. With that knowledge and experience, now apply bearing the pain to your own transgression. That transgression did happen. You cannot change that point in time, but you can alter your response to it, and one way of doing this is to bear the pain of what you did so that you do not . . .

- Keep punishing yourself
- Keep engaging in self-loathing
- Take out your pain on others
- Leave a legacy of pain in the world because at one point in your life, you were suffering great pain.

To bear pain is to stand with courage. When you bear the pain, you are no longer distracting yourself with worthless pursuits or undermining your own health because of a refusal to bear that pain. When you bear the pain, you are no longer a pain-giver, but a pain-bearer.

Try this visualization as a way to bear the pain from your own actions: Picture yourself sitting down and seeing a heavy sack which you do not want to pick up. It is filled with painful memories of disappointing yourself and others. Yet you now stand, take the pack, and place it onto your back. You are standing strong now. The pack is bearable and in fact is helping you to realize just how strong you are. As you hold this sack, you realize that the contents slowly shrink in size and weight. As you hold this sack, you are in essence protecting others from having to hold it, to bear it. In bearing the pain, you are a protector of others.

Who, then, are you as a person? Do you have inherent worth? Are you finally beginning to see this? Is it going deeply inside of you so that you embrace this truth about yourself?

Reminder 58:

When you can bear the pain of your own transgression, you become stronger.

Exercise #8: Giving Yourself a Gift as an Act of Mercy Toward Yourself

To forgive is to be merciful. To be merciful is to love. To love is to be a gift-giver. You have given gifts to others and now the point is to give a gift to yourself. What can you do for yourself (within reason, so that you do not become narcissistic, as Vitz and Meade warn) that is kind and gentle and loving? Think creatively here. For Jennifer, the gift was to begin thinking through a specific strategy for finally unburdening herself of her secret guilt. She would

approach her husband first and let him know of her unacceptable actions toward the company. After they worked
this through together, then the next step would be to give
the money back. She saw this as being good not just to
others but to herself as well.

The point is to welcome yourself back into the human
community in a genuine way. And let this welcoming be
more than a quick "Hello," only to banish yourself into the
outer darkness of the night once again. Can you, for example, take a little time to rest, or to start an exercise program, or to call a friend, or to reassure yourself that you
have great worth, or to get yourself ready for Exercise #11,
about making amends? Treat yourself to what you might
give to your best friend. You honor others. Now honor yourself—not because you are better than others or because
you are self-absorbed, just because you are worth it.

Exercise #9: What Are You Learning as You Are Self-Forgiving?

Forgiveness, including self-forgiveness, is a journey of discovery. Please reflect on these questions in your journal:
What are you discovering about yourself as you continue to
practice self-forgiveness? How have you changed? What is
your heart like now? Are you more welcoming of yourself?
More tolerant toward yourself? More loving toward yourself? More loving toward others?

As you develop the capacity to love yourself, extend
that service love to other people. With renewed energy,
use that love for the good of others. With the renewed
energy, begin to seek forgiveness and to make reparations
for your injustices, themes to which we turn now as we continue with the exercises.

Exercise #10: Seeking Forgiveness from Others

It's time for courage now to ask the hard question: "Who,
besides myself, was hurt by what I did?" As a reminder,
focus on the one situation that you identified at the begin-

ning of this key. You can turn to other issues after you finish with this one. There may be more than one person hurt. My point here is to focus on those directly and deeply hurt, not just mildly inconvenienced or even a little annoyed (which tends to vanish quickly).

1. A plan is helpful when seeking forgiveness, so that's the first task. Consider how you will seek the forgiveness: by electronic message, physical letter, phone, in-person talk? The best mode will depend on how you think the person will react. Sometimes people see the electronic route as indicating indifference, whereas others like its convenience and the time afforded to read, reread, and then respond. So try your best to serve the other by discerning the best mode of communicating your need and intention to be forgiven.

2. Compose the words or think through what you will say. Pedro decided to write a physical letter to his children. In it he started with a warm greeting and then expressed how badly he felt about the kind of father he had been. He explained in some detail what he had done so that the two children could understand clearly what his unrest was all about. He then asked them to forgive him. Here is an excerpt (which I am paraphrasing for the sake of privacy) of that letter:

> "I know that my asking you for your forgiveness may not be an easy thing to hear. I have not been with you and so we are emotionally distant. I own this and want to take responsibility for that and tell you how sorry I am. You may need time to think about this. You may respond with some initial anger and that is okay. In the long run, I hope that you will take my request seriously so that we can talk about the pain and begin to heal as a family. I love you and that is why I am taking the time to write to you and to take this risk of how you will respond to me. Thank you for considering my request."

3. As you ask for forgiveness from others, bear in mind that it is quite easy for people to misunderstand what it means to forgive. Thus, you should be clear about what you

are asking. You are not asking anyone to minimize what you did. You are not asking them to forget what happened or to just let it go. You are not saying that all is "okay." You are not even asking them to forgive immediately. As you know, it takes time when you are forgiving someone else. You are asking that those who were hurt begin to see your inherent worth, not because of what you did, but in spite of it. You are asking for mercy. Mercy, by its nature, is not deserved in the sense that you deserve justice from others. It is deserved in the sense that you are a person, and the one who was hurt by your actions is a person. You want to come together, when the other person is ready, face-to-face.

As a next step, be ready to practice humility if the response is not what you expected. You do not want this person's response to fuel anger in you so that this seeking of forgiveness degenerates into another feud. Instead, start now to prepare yourself for possible rejection of your offer. If the response is harsh and unfair, then consider forgiving how the other(s) responded, or failed to respond, to you. To prepare for this possibility, try to envision a rejection and how your heart will handle this. Envision what you will say and do if there is rejection. Be prepared.

4. Bear the pain of waiting. It is difficult when we open our heart to another or others and they are not ready to receive our offer. As you bear the painful uncertainty of waiting, you are actually aiding the recipient's possible forgiving response, and you are helping with your own emotional well-being. Pedro at first was unaware that he should practice bearing his pain once he sent the letter. His initial reaction, when neither child responded in the time he had expected, was a swelling of anger, which then led to anxiety. At that point, he was not ready to receive his children's response, whether it was positive or negative. Once he realized the necessity of bearing this pain, he strengthened inside and was better prepared to engage in the process of seeking and receiving forgiveness.

5. Be prepared to help the other(s) as he or she chooses

to enter the process of forgiveness. In many cases your apology will do a lot more than you might think to soften the hearts of those who are angry. The act of forgiving works more quickly and more smoothly when there is a sincere apology given at the beginning of the process of forgiving. Your allowing the others a time of anger also is important. Recall your own period of anger over some of the injustices you have faced. If this phase of anger was important for you, then it will likely be important for those now being asked to forgive you. Your patience will help the process of seeking and receiving forgiveness.

At some point in this process you may need to offer some gentle education on what inherent worth means and its importance for good interaction. This must be done delicately and with humility. Otherwise, it may look like you are trying to control their process of forgiving.

6. Finally, be aware of the unpredictability of seeking and offering forgiveness. These are not straight lines in which all people involved go quickly to the end and then all is well. Anger can reemerge. Some people need a time-out from the work. There may be misunderstandings that set the process back. Yet when good hearts take the time to accurately understand what forgiveness is and how to go about it, good things can happen, including reconciliation, even if there was estrangement for many years.

Reminder 59:

Seeking forgiveness from others takes humility and patience as you allow the other to forgive at his or her own pace.

Exercise #11: Working Toward Reparation or Other Forms of Justice

When you hurt yourself and others, the seeking of forgiveness is not a final step. Yes, there is a kind of triumph when both sides come to the "yes" of accepting each other as persons of worth. However, a step remains: It is now necessary for you to do your best to make up for what was taken away from the other(s).

Sometimes literal reparation is not entirely possible. In Pedro's case, he cannot take back "the stealing of time from his children" because he cannot go back in time to correct this fault. But he *can* do his very best now to be a good father and grandfather. He can, in a sense, make up some of that time now by his presence and love. All of them will have to walk together in life knowing that there is a wound from the past. That wound eventually will form into a scar that is part of the family history. It can serve as a reminder that there is both pain in the family *and* the courageous overcoming of that pain by a deliberate choice not to let it destroy the family.

Jennifer's case is complex in that she first has to seek forgiveness from her husband, from whom she hid her transgression for years. He might be angry about the secrecy and the difficult decision ahead of them about what to do regarding the company. Then will come the decision about the company itself.

When she confessed to her husband what she had done, he was troubled by it but did not berate or reject her. He showed more support than she had expected. Once they worked through their own issues, which took several weeks, they then devised a plan with the company. Rather than confess to the company directly, they decided together to give the money back, plus interest, to the company's philanthropic foundation. They sent a joint letter, without signing it, in which they offered an anonymous donation to the company's causes. They decided not to sign the letter so that they did not receive any unwarranted praise from the philanthropic foundation for giving the money. Both Jennifer and her husband were satisfied with this and she was able to unburden herself of years of debilitating guilt. She forgave herself, she sought and received forgiveness from her husband, and she gave back the money plus any interest the company lost as a result of the theft.

Reminder 60:

Trying to repair the effects of your injustice takes courage and creativity and can help set you free from guilt.

Questions about Self-Forgiveness

Question 1

"I have tried the exercises here and I still am unable to forgive myself. What now?"

As with the process of forgiving others, self-forgiveness takes both time and practice. If you are not experiencing some relief, the first step is to keep at it with regard to the situation you identified in Exercise #2. Then go to Exercises #5 and #6 and continue to do the work involving inherent worth and compassion.

If you are still having difficulty, see if you have left anyone out in this process of seeking forgiveness. Is there a person who is important to you, whom you hurt and have not asked for forgiveness? Take this inventory and then act accordingly. If you still need someone's forgiveness, this could be stalling your healing. Once he or she is identified, see what you need to do to make amends.

Question 2

"I agree with Vitz and Meade that self-forgiveness is not appropriate. Do you think that I can just seek forgiveness from others and make amends and not engage in all the rest of it?"

Yes, in your case, it seems that trying to go directly to seeking forgiveness from as many persons as necessary and making appropriate amends may be sufficient. There are many examples of people feeling emotionally better when doing these two and avoiding self-forgiveness exercises. Yet when this seeking of forgiveness and making amends is not enough, it is then that you might want to consider the exercises of self-forgiveness, but only if you choose. I have known people who have done just as you suggest with excellent results. I have known people who have done just as you suggest and cannot find inner peace until they do the work of self-forgiveness, with its exercises for reawakening one's own sense of inherent worth and practicing compassion toward the self (in addition to making amends with others).

Question 3

"Like Pedro, I have a cigarette habit. My doctor, while encouraging me to quit, realizes that quitting is not entirely under the control of my free will now. I have an addiction. Do I practice self-forgiveness when my behavior is not entirely under my own volition? In other words, I am not at this point choosing to do wrong."

Yes, you can self-forgive if you choose to do so. Here is why: When you made your choice to smoke cigarettes, you were not yet addicted. You actually did make a freely willed choice, which you acted upon. So you can forgive yourself for the choice that led to an addiction. Even now, you have choices within the context of the addiction such as smoking or not when others are in the room, whether or not to try a quit-smoking program, and how hard to work in that program. You *do* have free-will choices in the context of the addiction, and if you do not take full advantage of getting physically healthier, these behaviors are eligible for your self-forgiveness.

Question 4

"I tend to hurt myself over and over because of alcohol addiction. My father suffered from this malady, as did my grandfather. I watched as both of them sank into a kind of self-loathing as they failed to beat this disease. It is getting hard to keep forgiving my-self because I am losing patience with myself. What do you sug-gest?"

Although it may be fairly easy to forgive yourself for one offense that is not repeated, as you imply in the question, it gets harder when you keep letting yourself down. A central issue here is to keep forgiving yourself, even if it is on a daily basis, and never give up. Keep in mind all that self-forgiveness encompasses: seeking forgiveness from those whom you have hurt by your actions and making amends to those whom you have hurt by your actions. The seeking of forgiveness and the making of amends take courage.

When people engage in self-loathing, as your father and grand-father did, there can be a tendency not to work as hard at healthy responses to this challenge. It is a form of self-punishment, which in this case can do considerable harm both to you and to those affected by your behavior because you are not changing that behavior. As your anger toward yourself decreases through self-forgiveness, you are less likely to take that anger out on yourself by subconsciously subverting workable plans to stop alcohol use and to move toward greater health.

It is important that you realize that the addiction does include some free will on your part. You are not helpless in the face of this challenge. You could just throw up your hands if you take an extreme position that alcoholism is genetic with no room for per-sonal will and positive change. On the other hand, your taking an active role in confronting this condition, including self-forgiveness, could produce surprisingly positive results. A scientific study that my colleagues and I conducted with people in drug rehabilitation (mentioned in Key 1) showed strong and positive psychological improvements when they forgave others (not the self).[11] Because the processes of self-forgiveness and the forgiveness of others are similar, I would expect similar results when you self-forgive.

---

[11] Lin, W. F., Mack, D., Enright, R. D., Krahn, D., & Baskin, T. (2004). Effects of forgive-ness therapy on anger, mood, and vulnerability to substance use among inpatient substance-dependent clients. *Journal of Consulting and Clinical Psychology, 72*(6), 1114–1121. http://dx.doi.org/10.1037/0022-006X.72.6.1114; PMid:15612857

Self-Forgiveness and Your Future

Self-forgiveness is the time machine that allows you to go back and undo some of the harm your own actions have caused you and others. The exercises in this chapter are intended to give you confidence that relief from the guilt of breaking your own standards is possible. It's also important to realize that, as an imperfect person, you will disappoint yourself again in the future. You now have at your disposal a strong response to self-disappointment and even self-hatred. You are too important to lose time and energy on the lie that you are worthless. Continue to practice the thinking that you are special, unique, and irreplaceable, as is every person on the planet. This kind of thinking can serve as a protection for you when you let yourself down and when others let you down. We have focused much attention on *thinking* here. Let's now turn, in the final chapter, to issues of the *heart*.

DEVELOP THE HEART
OF FORGIVENESS

Is it possible that . . .

Forgiveness can awaken a sleeping world?
You can play a part in this awakening?
Even if people treat you like a stray cat and throw a shoe at you to
*   silence you . . . you continue to startle by loving?*
Others eventually might thank you for awakening them from their
*   Rip Van Winkle slumber?*
You will have a wide-awake new purpose for your life?
It is possible.

Are you ready to open the final door of the journey with Key 8? You might want to shield your eyes a bit as we open this door because it actually is brighter inside this room than it is outside. Love has a way of shining brightly. Love in the heart usually starts small and grows over time when practicing forgiveness. Love can give way to joy, experienced when you have faced cruelty and have overcome its challenging consequences. This kind of forgiveness does not come easily. It must be cultivated in the heart.

Much of our work to this point has focused on the mind of forgiveness, and now we enter the most important door of all with this final key. It unlocks the heart, the seat of our emotions according to ancient Greek teaching. The heart of forgiveness gets to the heart of your healing.

A Case Study to Open the Heart of Forgiveness

To help you forgive from the heart, let's first consider Avila's situation. Andreas, her former husband, abandoned the family 3 years ago. Before he left, he was very critical of her and at the same time very dissatisfied with himself.

Avila was aware of Andreas's problems with his father, who'd had little time for him when he was growing up. This lack of attention and caring from his father had affected Andreas's general sense of trust, but Avila thought that once they settled into their life together, he would relax, realize that she is on his side, and all would be well as he, she presumed, slowly built his trust. It was not to be.

Avila now was swimming in a sea of doubt. When she started the forgiveness process, she let a book on the topic of forgiveness sit on her nightstand for weeks. Whenever she caught a glimpse of that book, she immediately turned away, like an out-of-shape person might do as she enters the gym with all of those confusing machines smiling back at her, almost defying her to give them a try.

It was difficult for her when she started the forgiveness process because her own childhood training had conditioned her to think of forgiveness as some kind of mechanical formula, not a form of heart surgery leading to emotional healing. Her parents had enforced a kind of routine in which a parent demanded the offending child, "Say you're sorry," and then the other was instructed to accept this overture. It was a rote process that did not positively penetrate the children's hearts.

In time, Avila did the thinking level work that led her to the conclusion that Andreas is a person and therefore someone of inherent worth. She saw and sympathized with his emotional pain of not being able to trust. As she forgave him, and actually began to use that word, she did not see their entering back into the role of husband and wife together. Instead, she saw him as a valuable person, despite his actions.

Each day she took the time to think of Andreas as having this inherent worth as a person until slowly her heart began to soften toward him. Again, this was not so that she would pursue a marital relationship with him (because he was gone and showed no signs of returning), but instead it was to see how deeply wounded he is. After all, he gave up a loving wife, two wonderful children, and a life of caring, protection, and love. To throw away so much means that he has ruined a large part of his life. She was sad for him now rather than resentful. She stopped waking up in the middle of the night to lament the loss. She was able to let go of "what might have been" as her concern for Andreas-as-a-person grew.

What is particularly important about this growth of the heart is this: Avila never again said a bad word about Andreas, even unintentionally, to her children, Brigid and David. They were freed from the burden of taking sides. In fact, she spoke respectfully to them about Andreas, so that they could cultivate thoughts of respect toward their father, despite his flaws. Refraining from making disparaging remarks about Andreas was a loving gift from Avila to her children because she was giving their father back to them, in a psychological sense. Avila knows that in time, Andreas might try to win back his children's love so that he can spend time with them. Avila is laying the groundwork for this to happen by how she talks about Andreas. This, then, also is an indirect gift to Andreas.

In time, as Avila's love in her heart began to grow, she saw Andreas's father also as deeply wounded inside. This expanded view did not excuse his behaviors toward Andreas as a growing child, but it did shed more light on both of them as persons. They are both walking around with big holes in their hearts, and as a result, they are putting similar kinds of holes in others' hearts.

Although Avila started this forgiveness journey with no hope whatsoever, it slowly began to grow in her, becoming a source of encouragement. Hope for a better future now "put a smile in [her] heart" because she began to see that, without fairy-tale distortions, good things *can* happen for her. She had more energy to listen when her children were speaking to her. She was shedding the sense of being thrown down into a pit. She no longer felt like Eeyore in the Hundred Acre Wood, head down, voice low, proclaiming to herself that nothing ever works out. That "nothing ever works out" is one of the big lies. Although it is true that she did not get all that she wanted out of life, it is further true that the events of her life did not rob her of her inner world of love, mercy, forgiveness, and joy. She sees that she can stand in the hope that these inner qualities can be hers again, or even hers for the first time, as she practices forgiveness daily.

Exercise #1: Growing in Hope

Consider entertaining this thought: "I do not have to live with an inner world that is constantly nagging at me. I will not live with an inner world that is filled with negative thoughts and emotions. I can live my life from this moment onward so that my inner world makes more room for love, mercy, forgiveness, and joy, as Avila has. I have hope that I can accomplish this."

Type it and place it on your refrigerator, or in a desk drawer that you open frequently, or in your purse or backpack so that you can read and ponder this message several times a day.

Reminder 61:

Hope can and should be yours as you walk the path of forgiveness.

Continuing with Avila: The Generalization of Love

As hope began to be restored within her, Avila discovered, hidden away deep inside her, that love is a central part of who she is as a person. So often I see people who are beaten down by life, who forget this essential fact of existence: "I need to give and receive love as part of my humanity." Avila began to realize that she has experienced love as a conscious reality within her at some points in her life. She thought back to one incident in which her inner world was alive with joy, energy, and expectation because at least one person in this world was supporting and loving her. For her, it was the time that her father came home with her favorite sweets when, with a fever and fighting a virus, she was home from school. He sat on her bed and just talked about his day and truly wanted to know about her day. He was interested in her . . . as a person. That inner experience was and is very real within her, and no one can take that away.

Avila realized that just as she can, without wanting it or work- ing at it, slide into pessimism, she can, with some work, rekindle that inner liveliness of love—which no one can ever take away from her again. Sure, her love may have been stolen by a thief when she was not looking or suspecting, but because love is not an object like a purse or wallet, she always has it deep within, ready to be brought out and highlighted as a central part of her life.

Exercise #2: Showing Yourself That You Love and Are Loved

Think back to one time in which someone unconditionally loved you, not because of what you did, but because of who you are. *Who are you?* "I am someone who has loved and who has been loved. I am someone who is lovable and capable of giving great love to others. I have experienced love within and thus I know exactly what it is I am looking for." Please reflect on this at least once a day for the next week.

Reminder 62:

You are one who loves. It is part of who you are. Forgiveness can help you to love again.

Continuing with Avila: Love Is Stronger Than Any Injustices She Will Ever Face

The kind of love that Avila was cultivating in her heart is not the kind that is reciprocated by others, at least in the case of her former relationship with Andreas. She was giving where there was taking by the other. She was giving love in the face of another's lack of love and even abuse. This is so much harder to give than the kind of love that is reciprocated, such as giving love and support to a child who falls and hurts her knee and then embraces you as her protection in a painful world. Avila realized that it is so much more of a challenge when the other has decided that she is not as human as he or she is. It is then that her love was sorely tested.

And this kind of love takes practice, practice, *practice*. Avila had not practiced this kind of love in the little things, and so it was a great challenge to find this love as she groped for it in the darkness when abuse came. This is why it was so important for her to start the forgiveness journey so that eventually she would become what I call "forgivingly fit." She was ready to stand in forgiveness. And she triumphed. Are you ready to forgive from the heart?

Reminder 63:

Your love is stronger than any injustice that can ever come your way. You will have to do the work to let love be this strong in you.

Learning to Forgive from the Heart

With Key 3 (Identify the Source of Your Pain and Address Your Inner Turmoil) you identified people in need of your forgiveness. With Key 4 (Develop the Mind of Forgiveness) you first worked on forgiving one particular person for one particular injustice against you. Let's now deepen that forgiveness by adding the perspective of the heart. Keep this one person in mind, with the intent of forgiving others from the heart, as you complete the forgiveness work.

We start first with a preliminary examination of love specifically toward the one who hurt you before addressing more specific issues with him or her in the next exercise.

Exercise #3: Preparing to Practice Love as You Forgive

Do you need love in this world? The one who hurt you needs love, too. Love is something that goes beyond the physical. It is a need, a feeling, a set of actions, a set of thoughts that seem to lead many people into that which is eternal. Love connects people and motivates them to know each other deeply, to care, and to serve the other. Love goes beyond the physical heart, for example, in that once the body dies, the heart degenerates. Love, instead, continues after a person dies. Think about that for a moment: Even though a person dies, his or her love can remain on the earth as the recipients of that love carry loving attitude to others.

Do you need to give love? If you do not give love, what is your meaning and purpose in life? And is any meaning and purpose that lacks love truly satisfying for you? If you need to give love to be whole, so too does the one who hurt you. You share that in common.

The two of you share, in equal measure, the need to love and to be loved. You both need to transcend what you can experience with the senses to something greater. You share this kind of personhood. Do you think this is true or exaggerated? Please provide an answer in your journal.

Going Beyond Your Clearer Vision to Love as You Forgive

Let's now expand your clearer vision, which you developed using Key 4, by adding love as you forgive the one who had little or no love toward you. And please stand in love no matter what, no matter how much anyone ever withdraws love from you.

This is not an impossible task, even though it may seem so at first. You already have begun to *see* love. Use the *seeing* to help you move toward the *experiencing of love* in your heart. You already have begun to exercise love with Key 2 (Become Forgivingly Fit), and although it was toward those who have not withdrawn love from you, the point is that you have been exercising love. At this point in the journey, it's time to stretch yourself to a degree. You will not be doing something radically different, just doing the same thing in a more challenging context. Ten issues specifically concerning love in relation to the one who hurt you are addressed in the following exercise.

Exercise #4: Experiencing Standing in Love . . . for the One Who Hurt You

I suggest that you reflect in writing on each of the following 10 statements and questions. Do you agree or are there areas of disagreement? Try to be specific in your answers.

- *Love asks, "How may I serve you today?"* It's important to be realistic here because you are just beginning to grow in love toward those who are/were unfair to you. How can you serve this wounded, unhappy person today? Maybe you can say something nice about him to a friend. What does he need and how can you safely—*safely*—provide that in a small way?
- *Love builds up.* The one who hurt you likely had love withdrawn from her. How can you build up the person so that there is even a little love in her heart reservoir today? She truly needs this love, and she may not get it from anyone else today but you. Again, be safe and consider a way to let her wounded heart get a little love that is desperate for it. Even if the person is deceased, you can say a kind word about her to someone in the family.
- *Love refreshes others.* A smile refreshes. Acknowledgment that the one who hurt you is a person refreshes. You might wonder when he last truly felt himself to be a full-fledged person.
- *Love understands happiness.* Because you understand

happiness, can you see its reverse: the unhappiness in the other? You have the capacity to give this person even a little happiness. It is your choice. How will you do it? What will this moment of happiness do for her heart? What will this act of love do for your heart?

• *Love considers money to be a* means *to an end, not an end itself.* The point is not for you to give the person money. Instead the point is this: How can you help this person realize that the love of money (which is one concrete expression of power) is not the ultimate goal of his life? Money (not the love of it) is a means to certain more important goals. (If the person who hurt you is deceased, you cannot act on this one.)

• *Love is a bridge to others' betterment.* How can you be an example to this person, and to others, today so that she sees your love in action and is thereby helped to better understand love? You have the opportunity to provide a life-giving insight to this person. Exercise love today and possibly change a worldview . . . possibly change a life.

• *Love binds the wounds . . . even in the self.* By not being hostile, you could help ease this person's wounds, which he may have carried since childhood. A truce in a war gives each one time to bind wounds. Go even further than this and see what you can do to ease the unseen wounds in his heart.

Jonathan had a serious argument with his partner, Samantha. While she was out for a while, he unexpectedly cooked a meal for both of them. It was a complete surprise to her when she came home, weary because of the weight of the argument that she carried on her back and in her heart all day. The unexpected gift went a long way to mend the heart.

• *Love includes joy.* Joy in the context of injustice and forgiveness is that abiding sense of soaring love that we have overcome something heart-threatening or even life-threatening. We have survived and thrived through the chaos. It is possible that, over time, you could increase joy in the other's heart with this message: "Let's no longer enter a battle of the wounded hearts with each other. I am concerned about your heart and my heart. I want a whole and healthy heart for you. I want the same for myself."

• *Love understands power but is not impressed.* Keep the important focus that if the other person continues with a worldview of power (again, in its negative sense), then this can impact both of you. Resolve to see this exercise of power when it occurs and to *not* react to it with power. Keep justice before you. Keep love before you. Protect yourself, see with clearer vision, and stand in the truth that this is a person, a hurting person, who needs to hear of the worldview of love, and begin to practice it. It is a loving gesture to want a worldview of love for him.

• *Love endures even in the face of grave power against it.* If you are able to ignite even the smallest spark of love in the other person, how can you help to keep that spark going? If she does not get such encouragement from others, then it is possible that the little spark may be quickly extinguished. How can you help prevent that from happening? You may be one of the few people on the planet who could help this person not only to grow in love but also to persevere in it.

What are the sources of power that are impinging on this person's heart, stifling love? Are you in a position to have a discussion with her about these sources of power that rob her of happiness? Having such a conversation requires courage. It also requires wisdom because you do not want to do this if it will start a fire of controversy and discontent between you. Proceed with such a discussion only if it is safe.

If none of this is possible and if she has chosen to exercise power rather than love, then it is time to protect your own heart. And remember that you can love from a distance when the circumstances require distance.

Reminder 64:

You can love . . . even those who have not loved you.

Questions about Forgiving with Love

Question 1

"I'm not ready to add love to the other keys to forgive the person who hurt me. Does this make my forgiveness incomplete?"

The word *incomplete* could refer to your own emotional healing. In this case, you can experience considerable emotional healing without trying to love the other person. We have not done studies that deliberately compare "forgiveness with love" and "forgiveness without love," and so I cannot be entirely sure what the difference is for your emotional well-being. Yet I am confident that not all of the people whom my colleagues and I have helped over the years have forgiven with love in their hearts, and still we find excellent results for emotional health when they forgive (by reporting to our research team, for example, that they sense inside of them that they have forgiven).

The word *incomplete* could refer to the process of forgiveness itself. In this case, you are not reaching the deepest end point of forgiveness, and that is all right if your immediate goal is emotional relief. People often end our intervention programs with some anger left over and without a high score on our forgiveness measure. Nonetheless, they experience significant emotional healing.

Question 2

"Saying that the other person is wounded from the past seems to me to be making excuses for the unfair behavior. I am to forgive because someone was bad to him. Well, he was bad to me. Doesn't he have to just 'man up,' as they say, and stop the insensitivity and hurt?"

To see the injurer's wounds from his past is not to excuse his hurtful behavior but instead to see him in a new way. As you see those wounds, you are not making the unjust behavior suddenly just. You need to keep both forgiveness *and* justice in mind at the same time. If your call is for him only to stop the behavior, then you are focusing only on the issue of justice, not mercy. The process of forgiveness asks you to focus simultaneously on both mercy and justice. When you do, you are not ignoring the injustice and you are not ignoring the self-chosen response of mercy.

Exercise #5: Who Are You When You Love?

You can and do love. You have been offering love to strangers, acquaintances, loved ones, and now even toward those who are difficult to love (because they have not loved you). Try reading this affirmation several times a day: "I can love. I am someone who is a bridge to love for others. I have within my will the ability and resolve to offer love in a world that understands power to a far greater extent than it understands love."

You are not what those who injure you say you are. They have been telling you lies. They might not have deliberately lied to you. As they see through the lens of power, the world gets all twisted around for them. You can be a straightener of the twisted. So, then, who are you? Tell your story of who you are to yourself. Don't hold back on the love part. It is central to who you are becoming.

Question 3

"I have heard it said many times that 'love is a decision, not a feeling.' Is this true?"

Love, as we are considering it here, is a moral virtue, as is mercy and patience and kindness. All moral virtues are engaged by the entire person, not just one aspect of that person. Yes, to love is to decide to stand firm in the loving even when you do not feel like it. So the will is very important here. At the same time, as you grow in love, you will see that it is more than a decision. It is a *set of actions that aids the other.* It includes feelings that could be described as compassion and caring, no matter how small these are in your heart right now. And it is about your identity—about who you are as a person. To say, "I am a loving person," and know that this is true about you is part of what love is.

Reminder 65:

You are a person who loves, even in the face of grave power attacks against you.

Question 4

"I'm afraid that I will get 'used up' if I love. There will be nothing left of me. What do you think?"

The paradox of service love is that as you extend mercy to those who have had no mercy on you, it is *you* who experiences emotional healing. The scientific studies on forgiveness therapy and education in Key 1 made this point. If you are insincere in your "loving" and do this only for yourself, then, yes, emotional burnout could happen. It's important to guard against such a perspective and its possible consequence of burnout. When you decide to love, make a distinction between what this love is (being in service to others) and the consequences of such love (you begin to feel better). If you make this distinction and practice service love accordingly, then, as seen in our science, you will be moving toward greater, not lesser, emotional well-being.

Exercise #6: A Heart Check: How Are You Progressing in Your Emotional Healing?

It's time to check your heart with regard to your general state of psychological health. As you may recall from Key 3, you used a scale of 1–5 to rate the degree to which you were feeling inner pain. Once again answer the following seven statements by rating each on a scale of 1–5, as follows (and if you need a refresher on the meaning of any of the following terms, reread the descriptions in Key 3, pp. 76–84):

1 = not at all
2 = to a small extent
3 = to a moderate extent
4 = to a large extent
5 = to an extreme extent

1. I'm anxious.
2. I'm depressed.
3. I have unhealthy anger inside of me.
4. I lack trust in other people.
5. I don't like myself.
6. My worldview is negative.
7. I don't think that I will be able to overcome my wounded inner world.

How did you score this time, relative to how you scored in Key 3? Go back to those scores and compare each one with your present score. If you gave a rating of 4 or 5 to any one of these statements, then you need to continue doing the work of healing your inner world. As you now know, the higher the score, the more pervasive are your wounds. By way of quick review, the scale ranges from a low score of 7 to a high score of 35. A high score of 5 on anxiety, depression, unhealthy anger, and self-esteem suggests that you should consider getting professional help for the symptoms.

Continue to let love grow in you as you examine now-familiar themes, but this time with love added to each. We will start with what we have called your worldview: your sense of how the world works.

Exercise #7: Knowing Your Worldview

Use your journal, whether hard copy or electronic, to answer the following questions. Don't try to answer them all at one time. Take all the time you need to explore who you are with the help of these questions:

What is your worldview now? How does the world work?

Begin writing your story: Who are you and where are you going in life?

Based on your answer to the question above, who are people in general? What is the essence of a human being?

What is important to you in this world?

What are your short-term goals in the next year?

What are your long-term goals for when you look back at the end of your life?

What will you want to have accomplished?

How will you serve others who have suffered?

Finding Your New Meaning in Overcoming

With Key 5 we talked about finding meaning in *suffering*. Making meaning is a key to healing that Viktor Frankl brought to the world's attention after his grave suffering during World War II. The meaning we find in suffering is different from the meaning we experience once we triumph by overcoming the suffering. The next exercise further explores this topic.

Exercise #8: Finding Meaning by Growing in Love

Did you have as deep an understanding and appreciation of love before you suffered the loss of love from someone else's unfair treatment of you? Were you aware that forgiveness is the aikido that defeats meanness and cruelty, that overthrows power with love? Why forgive? Because forgiveness defeats meanness and cruelty and makes the growth of love possible.

As you strive to find meaning in this life by practicing love more willingly and deeply, you will have to cultivate two moral qualities that do not seem to go together so easily in this world: humility and courage. Sometimes humility is seen as a sheepish trait, only for the weak. Sometimes courage is seen as an overpowering quality, only for the strong. Yet, as you love more, the combination of humility and courage is likely to grow in you. Humility helps you to see the equality of all persons through your clearer vision. Courage helps you to move forward in love in the face of a world that does not understand love. Remember this idea from Key 3: Power does not understand love, but love understands power. Your suffering might help deepen this insight in you and strengthen your resolve to move forward with love. And so to these questions:

- Do you see the importance of humility in overcoming the effects of injustice and suffering? If so, why is humility important?
- Do you see the importance of fostering courage as you overcome? If so, why is courage important?
- Do you see the importance of fostering love as you overcome? Why or why not?

Reminder 66:

Your suffering can play a part in a more mature understanding of what it means to be humble, courageous, and loving.

Exercise #9: Finding Meaning in the Insight That You Have Goodness to Offer Because You Have Suffered

For this exercise, I pose a series of questions for your reflection in your journal. Please take your time with this exercise because it requires some deep thought.

How has your suffering shown you your own strength to

be good, despite what has been thrown onto you? Are you beginning to see that your suffering has made you an even better person than before: stronger, wiser, more compassionate, with even more to offer to a hurting world than before you suffered?

Do you now have a strengthened inner resolve—calmer in the face of injustice, more resolute in knowing what is right and wrong, firmer in standing against injustice? Do you see important meaning to life if you live it this way?

What meaning do you make of your life when you deliberately live it in service to others, including the offering of love to those who have hurt you? Is life richer for you, filled with more interesting days? Has the suffering brought out for you the importance of service to others?

Has your suffering helped you to understand and appreciate forgiveness itself on deeper levels? Perhaps your suffering has opened you to this new, life-giving virtue in a way that you now see the beauty of forgiveness.

And for those of you who are religious, has your suffering and the overcoming of it changed your relation to the divine, the higher power, as some say? Bitterness has a way of turning you away from the divine. Some turn on the divine because other people turned on them. When treated cruelly by a father, for example, some people become angry with God when the theme of Father is part of the theology. Overcoming the suffering can reverse this and add meaning to faith rather than create one more division inside of a person.

Questions on Worldview and Finding Meaning

Question 5

"I am having a hard time seeing what the difference is between forming a worldview and finding meaning in suffering. Can you clarify this for me?"

A person's worldview answers the large questions of life such as:

"What are humans like at their very core?"
"Is there a purpose to my life?"
"Where will I go, if anywhere, when I die?"

Finding meaning does not necessarily address these large questions but instead centers on figuring out relevance, for oneself and others, within the suffering that helps one to endure and even to thrive. The one who is finding meaning in suffering often asks questions of practicality and service such as this: "How can I apply, in a practical way, what I am learning here for my own good and the good of others?" The person who is expanding his or her worldview might ask, "Now how does all of this fit into the way the world works and who people are?" Of course, one can go to the large questions when trying to find relevance while suffering, but this is not always the case. Here is an example of finding meaning that extends to the large questions of life, in this case for the religious person: "Why is God allowing me to suffer now?" The religious person, by asking this question, is beginning to ask about the qualities of the divine. Yet even the answer to this question does not explicitly and deliberately address the even larger worldview question of what people are like as humans and what God is like. These questions are part of formulating a worldview.

Question 6

"What if I decide that life is meaningless. Isn't standing in the truth of this more important than making up some kind of meaning just to reduce suffering? Then I would be trading in truth for comfort, which would diminish me."

Some philosophers have discussed a perspective that they call *nihilism*, in which there is nothing to which life is pointing: There is no real purpose in life and there is no real meaning beyond meaninglessness. But I wonder if they are living a contradiction. One of their purposes in life surely is to bring the message to others that there is no purpose and meaning in life. This is a goal, and goals point to purposes. Even to say that life has no meaning is to deliberately foster in oneself a meaning that life has no meaning. The philosophy of nihilism would seem more legitimate to me if those fostering it would just pull the blanket up over their heads and not try to convert others to the idea. As soon as they get out of bed and start talking to others about their new philosophy, then they are living a contradictory life.

And even if my ideas above are dismissed, we still have this problem: If nothingness or nihilism is seen as a truth, then we have another contradiction: The one with this idea sees that there is truth, and so one *purpose* in life is to seek the truth. One *meaning* in life is that there is truth to be understood. And so nihilism once again collapses in upon itself.

New Life Purposes After Forgiving

As you forgive, your purpose in life—why you are here and then acting on this—may develop. Purpose is different from finding meaning. When you find meaning in the context of injustice, this is a *thinking exercise* as you try to figure out the importance that suffering and its aftermath have for you. When you cultivate purpose, this is more *action-oriented* as you bring good things to others. I see nine different purposes to life once people begin to take forgiveness seriously. Let's examine each as a way of helping you decide what your new purposes in life might be.

Exercise #10: Examining Your New Purposes in Life

Nine "purposes" are introduced here. Which of them resonates with you so that you might want to make them a part of your life? Once you choose some of these, please write in your journal the concrete ways that you can fulfill the purposes.

Purpose 1: To Practice Forgiveness in a Loving Way as an End in Itself Because It Is Good

Part of your new life now can be to practice forgiveness often, as it becomes a part of who you are. Forgiveness can be part of your new way of seeing, part of your new actions toward others, and part of your heart. You now can begin to see all people as possessing inherent worth. You can respond to each person whom you meet from now on with a respect for him or her as a person. You can cultivate forgiving love in your heart as a way of life . . . just because. Is this one of your purposes in life now?

Purpose 2: To Protect Loved Ones from Your Emotional Wounds

Forgiveness offers protection to your loved ones when you are the one who is hurt. How is this possible? When you are all bottled up inside with resentment and anger, you can throw all of that unprocessed emotion onto others. You stop displacing anger before it starts as you deliberately choose forgiveness for the purpose of protecting others from that anger.

Reminder 67:

Your forgiveness protects your loved ones' emotional well-being.

Purpose 3: To Help the Person Who Is Unjust See the Error of His or Her Ways

The protection of forgiveness can even be extended to the one who hurt you. As you practice forgiveness, you do not toss your anger back at the one behaving badly. And, as you refrain from tossing the resentment back to the other, your restraint prevents the injurer's retaliation and a never-ending battle of wills that leads nowhere but to deeper pain. As you forgive, you prevent the escalation of further anger building up in you and in the injurer. In a way this is a gift to the one who hurt you because you are deliberately taking steps not to hurt him or her. Forgiveness has a certain nobility to it as you stand for peace when you could be exchanging angry glances or words.

Reminder 68:

Your forgiveness protects the one who hurt you.

Purpose 4: To Help the Other Grow in Character

The point here is not that you are exercising power over the other by showing your fine character in contrast to your injurer's character flaws. Instead, the point is that you have an opportunity to help someone overcome his or her hurtful ways—the ways that led to your misery. As you show love for your injurer, you may be opening a door that has not been unlocked for a long time. Showing this key, the heart of forgiveness, to your injurer could change his or her life.

Purpose 5: To Reconcile with Him or Her

As you understand the depth of forgiveness, you are able to see that to reconcile involves forgiving and the seeking and receiving of forgiveness. You see more clearly what the injustice is and what needs changing if you and your injurer are to come together again in mutual trust. One of your purposes, as you forgive, is to work toward that reconciliation to the extent that it is possible. If the injurer refuses, know that you have done your best. Even the offer of love and a more peaceful relationship will not move some people. You are not responsible for his or her actions or choices.

Purpose 6: To Grow in Character Yourself

The quest to become forgivingly fit has a way of being not just a "full-body workout" but also a "full-person workout." As you forgive, you will see that one of your purposes in life is to continue growing in virtues such as justice, patience, and kindness. You will see that you do not practice each virtue in its own little box but that they all work together for good. Don't be surprised that as you become forgivingly fit, growth in these virtues occurs as well.

Purpose 7: To Create an Atmosphere of Forgiveness in the Home

You will not want to keep forgiveness a secret as you practice it often. You will want to give it away. What better place to start than within your own family? Allow time for family members to discuss forgiveness. Be aware of teachable moments about it. For example, suppose that as a family you have watched a film and are now discussing it. You could bring up instances in the film in which one character might have considered forgiveness and how the plot of the story would have changed if this had occurred. Allow a time to discuss injustices suffered outside the home this week and how the different family members employed forgiveness as part of the response. Think creatively here. There are many ways of bringing forgiveness to the family so that it becomes a norm within it.

Purpose 8: To Create an Atmosphere of Forgiveness in the Workplace, in Worship Communities, and in Social or Other Communities

Not only does forgiveness protect your emotional health, your loved ones' well-being, and the one who hurt you, but also it protects the various communities in which you participate: your local community and those areas of community in which you spend much time, such as the workplace, your chosen house of worship, and/or social or political groups. Think about the trail of anger left when one person, acting alone and seemingly in isolation, lets loose in the family context with sneers and jibes and disrespect and temper tantrums. All of this starts in one heart and goes to the partner and the children and the grandparents when they come to visit. All of this then is transported into the workplace and by the children into the school and by the parents to their own communities. Discontent then emerges in a work colleague or in the back of the worship space as grumblings occur—all because of this first outpouring of discontent by one lone person in one small place in the universe—and it spreads far and wide to such an extent that no one knows its origin or knows how to put it back in the bottle. Anger spreads, sometimes indiscriminately. When forgiveness is in the heart of this one, lone actor in the world, this trajectory of anger is averted . . . quietly, anonymously, and without trumpets or fanfare. It prevents what could be destructive anger that spreads.

Reminder 69:

Your forgiveness can protect your communities from experiencing your unhealthy anger.

Purpose 9: To Protect Future Generations from Unhealthy Anger

And there is still more protection that occurs when forgiveness is practiced as a lifestyle. Your anger literally could continue to exist for years as it is passed along the generations to unsuspecting others. Anger is like a virus not only in spreading to other people in the present but also in its transmission across time . . . even a *long* time. When this unhealthy anger expresses itself in schools, principals and teachers have a name for this: *bullying*. The bullying of one child may well have started with some aggressive action hidden deep in a family and then it just spread, like a virus, to others inside and outside of that home. A child who is bullied might then inflict that bullying behavior onto a child in an earlier grade, who passes it to a child in an even earlier grade. A child born today could be the recipient of this passed-along anger in this school 5 years from now as he enters school for the first time. The anger will be waiting there to greet him, living in the heart of a child bullied by another, who was bullied by another, who was mistreated at home years before. Forgiveness can stop this generational transmission of anger and protect others from all of this unnecessary pain.

At our International Forgiveness Institute in Madison, Wisconsin (internationalforgiveness.com), we have developed 17 different curriculum guides for teachers and parents to use for instructing children and adolescents in the art of forgiveness. There is a complete set of guides from pre-kindergarten (age 4) through the senior year in high school (ages 17 and 18), an anti-bullying guide for middle school and early high school (ages 10 to 14), and two guides for parents. These are now being used on every continent in the world except for Antarctica (are there schools in Antarctica?). We have done research on these programs in which a teacher instructs a classroom of students for about 30–45 minutes a week for 12–15 weeks (depending on the age of students). The research shows a decrease in unhealthy anger in children as they learn about forgiveness through storybooks and short novels. This then becomes part of teachers' purposes: to give the children the protection of forgiveness and the gift of reduced anger.[12]

Will you be one who fosters the spread of the anger virus, or is your forgiveness practice the antidote, the cure, for the spread of

---

[12] Enright, R. D., Knutson, J. A., Holter, A. C., Baskin, T., & Knutson, C. (2007). Waging peace through forgiveness in Belfast, Northern Ireland II: Educational programs for mental health improvement of children. *Journal of Research in Education*, Fall, 63–78; Gambaro, M. E., Enright, R. D., Baskin, T. A., & Klatt, J. (2008). Can school-based forgiveness counseling improve conduct and academic achievement in academically at-risk adolescents? *Journal of Research in Education*, 18, 16–27; Holter, A. C., Magnuson, C., Knutson, C., Knutson Enright, J. A., & Enright, R. D. (2008). The forgiving child: The impact of forgiveness education on excessive anger for elementary-aged children in Milwaukee's central city. *Journal of Research in Education*, 18, 82–93; Enright, R. D., Rhody, M., Litts, B., & Klatt, J. S. (2014). Piloting forgiveness education in a divided community: Comparing electronic pen-pal and journaling activities across two groups of youth. *Journal of Moral Education*, 43, 1–17.

the anger disease? It really is your choice. Your seemingly isolated acts of frustration, discouragement, and unhealthy anger do have consequences—for others—across a long span of time. Likewise, your seemingly isolated acts of forgiveness *do* have positive consequences—for others—across a long span of time.

Reminder 70:

Your forgiveness now can protect future generations from unhealthy anger.

In the End: The Love in Your Heart Can Lead to Joy

Once you are able to reintroduce yourself to love . . . once you develop some of those purposes in life discussed above . . . you will find a kind of abiding sense of well-being in your heart that you may eventually identify as joy. One synonym for joy is *triumph*. Once you have overcome the meanness or indifference or even cruelty of others, you will know that you have triumphed. All of these attempts to steal your humanity have not worked. You are left . . . triumphant. When this realization dawns in your heart, you know that you will never be defeated by others' unhappiness. As you live with this realization—*live* with it, not just temporarily feel something good—you will have joy.

You may not be there yet. I would be very surprised if you were, because achieving this steady state of joy takes time and the practice of forgiveness. I am pointing it out to you now so that your hope can increase, which may foster more love in you— which in turn produces joy. Be patient and at the same time keep your eyes fixed on this important end point of forgiveness: *joy* . . . not just for you, but as a goal for others as well.

Reminder 71:

Joy can be yours for the first time or reignited in you . . . and then given to others.

Leaving a Legacy of Love on This Earth

Each one of you reading this book and I as the author share the fact that one day we will die. What will you leave behind to others on this earth when you are gone? If you make a commitment to bear your pain and not pass it on to others, this would be an important first step in the formation of your legacy. Then making a commitment to give love to others, even to those who have wounded you, would be an important second step in transforming your legacy into one of love.

Think about this: Long after you are gone, your love could be alive and well and living on this earth in the minds, hearts, and beings of others. You can begin to leave a legacy of love by how you live this very day. In all likelihood, you will meet others today. If your heart is filled with love rather than with bitterness, it will be much easier to pass that love to others.

Do you see why it is so important to forgive? You are given the joyous opportunity to shed bitterness and put love in its place for the one who hurt you and then more widely to many, many others, as you are freed to love more deeply and more widely. The meaning and purpose of your life are intimately tied to this decision to leave a legacy of love.

The Night Is Far Gone . . . Soon It Will Be Morning

You have suffered, perhaps through what some call the dark night of the soul. You have not deserved the darkness. I want you to know that the night is far gone in that you already have endured a time of great pain and now you are walking toward the light of deep forgiveness, love, and, yes, even joy. The darkness is not forever. Sometimes we have to fight our way out of that darkness, as you have in this book. Your path has been one of moving ever closer to the light that is forgiveness.

Stand for a while in the warm sun and feel it on your face.

Abide in the warmth. That warmth is the beginning of love in your heart that can radiate throughout all of you, into the world, and right into the hearts of others . . . many others . . . for many years to come.

It is time. You have suffered long enough. Come into the warmth and light of love that grows richer, more meaningful, and more joyous as you embrace the world of forgiveness with its mercy and truth and goodness and beauty. With forgiveness, you never have to leave the light ever again. I do not mean that suffering will never come again. I do mean that when it comes, it cannot throw you back to the darkness where there is bitterness mingled with doubt about who you are.

You know who you are now. You are a person who has endured much and who is standing. You are a person who has seen what power unleashed can do in this world. You have seen how forgiveness can meet that power head on and with gentleness eliminate the effects of it, the darkness, despair, and hopelessness that imprison your heart. No more. You now know the path. You know the eight resting places. Keep the map handy so that you never, ever forget who you are and where you are going in this challenging life.

Reminder 72:

Forgiveness as surgery for your heart can save your life . . . and the lives of others.

REMINDERS ABOUT
THE REMINDERS

All of your reminders are listed below as a way to review the journey of forgiveness. The list is a quick summary of the entire book. (For those of you who have not read the book yet, this is not "the forgiveness pill," in that, if you read the reminders, you quickly forgive and heal emotionally.) The list is for readers who have walked the forgiveness path in this book, who have used each of the keys, done the exercises, and know the depth behind each reminder. Read, review, and continue the healing.

Reminder 1: Science supports the view that you can be emotionally healed from the unfair situation or situations that have been a part of your life. Forgiveness can help bring about this kind of healing for you.

Reminder 2: Forgiveness of others is a protection for your own emotional well-being and for how you view who you are as a person.

Reminder 3: Your forgiveness can lead to more orderly thinking, feeling, and acting.

Reminder 4: Your forgiveness can be so strong that it helps you minimize disorder.

Reminder 5: Your forgiveness can help you stand against the worst kind of injustice so that it does not defeat you.

Reminder 6: When you forgive, you have mercy on those who have been unjust to you. You may or may not reconcile with the one who acted unjustly.

Reminder 7: Many people find that making the commitment to forgive is the hardest part of the journey.

Reminder 8: Each person is special, unique, and irreplaceable. It takes time and effort to understand this fundamental point.

Reminder 9: Service love is the kind of love in which the person gives of the self to others. It takes time and practice to get to such a point in one's life.

Reminder 10: Mercy is a variant of service love that is extended to the person who has caused you pain and takes patience and effort to master.

Reminder 11: Pride and power can get in the way of your forgiving. They can get in the way of positively transforming who you are as a person.

Reminder 12: Power and love vie for your attention.

Reminder 13: You can practice clearer vision and service love toward other people whenever you want.

Reminder 14: You can respond to minor annoyances with the Big Three of clearer vision, service love, and mercy.

Reminder 15: Forgiveness can fade in you to where you no longer even think about it. Do yourself and others a favor by not letting that happen.

Reminder 16: Persevering in your forgiveness practice may be one of your greatest and most rewarding challenges throughout your life.

Reminder 17: There is healing for your pain through the practice of forgiveness if you choose to be healed.

Reminder 18: We all have rights and obligations. Those who pull away your rights are being unjust.

Reminder 19: Obligations can be broken deliberately or passively without the person intending it. In either case, a broken obligation damages your rights.

Reminder 20: The other's worldview of power can result in injustices toward you in the false name of goodness. Don't be fooled by his or her argument that you were not treated unjustly.

Reminder 21: When you use the lens of power, you distort what is and what is not an injustice against you. You can too easily accuse others of injustices that are not injustices. Shed the lens of power to have clearer vision.

Reminder 22: When someone is unjust to you, the consequences can be very damaging for you. You have a right to fix those consequences, especially those internal consequences that I call *inner turmoil*.

Reminder 23: Forgiveness is good in and of itself.

Reminder 24: From a psychological perspective, forgiveness is a good practice in which to engage because it can heal the person who was wounded. This does not make forgiveness a self-serving activity when we focus on the consequences of injustice and want to heal from them.

Reminder 25: You can overcome the negative circumstances in your life from being treated unfairly, using forgiveness as the antidote.

Reminder 26: The way a person lives his or her life now will have consequences for his or her well-being much later in life. A person who wounds others now may feel the effects of this in his or her elderly years.

Reminder 27: At the time of the injury, the person who hurt you probably was carrying significant wounds. They are now yours. What will you do with them?

Reminder 28: You share a common personhood with the one who hurt you.

Reminder 29: The person who hurt you is more than those wounds imposed on you.

Reminder 30: You grow stronger as you see the one who hurt you as a wounded person, as someone who needs healing for those wounds.

Reminder 31: You are growing in your efforts to become forgivingly fit. You just have to keep at it to maintain the fitness.

Reminder 32: Meaning gives hope to the suffering you have experienced and may ultimately bring joy into your life.

Reminder 33: To find meaning in what you have suffered is a path out of discouragement and despair and into greater hope.

Reminder 34: As you make new goals in light of what you have suffered, you are adding new meaning to your life.

Reminder 35: Your suffering can help you to see the truth about what is just and unjust.

Reminder 36: Your suffering can help you realize that you will not let the badness in this world rob you of your goodness . . . for the good of others.

Reminder 37: Your suffering has not been for nothing. It can make you more attuned to the goodness within you.

Reminder 38: Your suffering can be a means of making you stronger.

Reminder 39: If you choose, you will begin today to see beauty rather than only the darkness and you will never let the darkness win.

Reminder 40: Your inner qualities of beauty are brought forth by your suffering.

Reminder 41: As you give service to others with wounded hearts, your heart begins to heal.

Reminder 42: Suffering can add to your knowledge of what forgiveness is. Suffering can aid you in becoming a more forgiving person and in seeking forgiveness from others.

Reminder 43: Try to see what your faith tradition says about suffering and the overcoming of suffering as an opportunity for you to grow as a person.

Reminder 44: Forgiveness and justice "grow up" together, so never toss either one aside.

Reminder 45: When suffering intensifies, know that this is not your final state. Forgiveness eventually leads to a reduction in the internally felt suffering and in the negative aftereffects of that suffering.

Reminder 46: You need not fear "looking suffering in the eye" because forgiveness is a safety net for you. Forgiveness can protect you from the heart-wounds of suffering and make you stronger.

Reminder 47: Despite being hurt by another, you can continue to realize that you are a person of great worth and that this worth cannot be taken away from you.

Reminder 48: When you take a long perspective on your troubles, you see that you will be at a different point in your life one year from now.

Reminder 49: The combination of humility and courage helps you to avoid excessive self-criticism and excessive criticism of others.

Reminder 50: Having a strong will helps you to continue to forgive even when you are tired and want to walk away.

Reminder 51: As you bear the pain of what happened to you, you may be protecting others and future generations from your anger.

Reminder 52: *Sacrifice* is a *reaching out* to the other, within reason, even when it is uncomfortable to do so.

Reminder 53: If you have believed in a higher power, do not turn against the higher power because someone turned against you.

Reminder 54: The warnings that self-forgiveness is either inappropriate or psychologically dangerous seem to focus more on false forms of it than on self-forgiveness itself.

Reminder 55: Self-forgiveness includes seeking forgiveness and making reparation toward those who were hurt by your actions (which also hurt you).

Reminder 56: When you offend yourself, you might lose your own sense of inherent worth. It is time to reclaim the truth: You are a person of inherent worth.

Reminder 57: See yourself as you are: as a person who is worthy of your time and respect and compassion, no matter what.

Reminder 58: When you can bear the pain of your own transgression, you become stronger.

Reminder 59: Seeking forgiveness from others takes humility and patience as you allow the other to forgive at his or her own pace.

Reminder 60: Trying to repair the effects of your injustice takes courage and creativity and can help set you free from guilt.

Reminder 61: Hope can and should be yours as you walk the path of forgiveness.

Reminder 62: You are one who loves. It is part of who you are. Forgiveness can help you to love again.

Reminder 63: Your love is stronger than any injustice that can ever come your way. You will have to do the work to let love be this strong in you.

Reminder 64: You can love . . . even those who have not loved you.

Reminder 65: You are a person who loves, even in the face of grave power attacks against you.

Reminder 66: Your suffering can play a part in a more mature understanding of what it means to be humble, courageous, and loving.

Reminder 67: Your forgiveness protects your loved ones' emotional well-being.

Reminder 68: Your forgiveness protects the one who hurt you.

Reminder 69: Your forgiveness can protect your communities from experiencing your unhealthy anger.

Reminder 70: Your forgiveness now can protect future generations from unhealthy anger.

Reminder 71: Joy can be yours for the first time or reignited in you . . . and then given to others.

Reminder 72: Forgiveness as surgery for your heart can save your life . . . and the lives of others.

Suggested Reading

Dalai Lama, & Chan, V. (2005). *The wisdom of forgiveness*. New York: Riverhead Books. [This book is from the Buddhist tradition.]

Enright, R. D. (2001). *Forgiveness is a choice*. Washington, DC: APA Books. [This book is for the general public and is a psychological approach to forgiveness.]

Enright, R. D. (2004). *Rising above the storm clouds*. Washington, DC: Magination Press. [An imprint of the American Psychological Association. This is a children's picture book on forgiveness with notes for parents.]

Enright, R. D. (2012). *The forgiving life*. Washington, DC: APA Books. [This book is for the general public, based on a psychological approach, and gives a broader view of forgiveness than the book, *Forgiveness is a choice*.]

Enright, R. D. (2012). *Anti-bullying forgiveness program: Reducing the fury within those who bully*. Madison, WI: International Forgiveness Institute. [This is a guide for school counselors and psychologists. This is for students between the ages of 11 and 14. It can be found on the website: internationalforgiveness.com.]

Enright, R. D., & Fitzgibbons, R. (2015). *Forgiveness therapy*. Washington, DC: APA Books. [This book is for helping professionals.]

Enright, R. D., & Knutson Enright, J. A. (2010). *Reaching out through forgiveness: A guided curriculum for children, ages 9–11*. Madison, WI: International Forgiveness Institute. [This is the fourth grade curriculum for teachers and parents (for students ages 9–11). There are 17 such guides for children from age 4 to adolescents age 18. These can be found on the website: internationalforgiveness.com.]

Klein, C. (1997). *How to forgive when you can't forget*. New York: Berkley. [This book is from the Jewish tradition.]

Smedes. L. B. (2007). *Forgive & forget*. New York: HarperOne. [This book is from the Protestant Christian tradition.]

Worthington, E. L., Jr. (Ed.) (2005). *Handbook of forgiveness*. New York: Routledge. [This book is for academics seeking a broad view of forgiveness.]

Bibliography

Enright, R. D., Knutson, J. A., Holter, A. C., Baskin, T., & Knutson, C. (2007). Waging peace through forgiveness in Belfast, Northern Ireland II: Educational programs for mental health improvement of children. *Journal of Research in Education*, Fall, 63–78.

Enright, R. D., Rhody, M., Litts, B., & Klatt. J. S. (2014). Piloting forgiveness education in a divided community: Comparing electronic pen-pal and journaling activities across two groups of youth. *Journal of Moral Education*, 43, 1–17. doi: 10.1080/03057240.2014.888516

Fitzgibbons, R. P. (1986). The cognitive and emotive uses of forgiveness therapy in the treatment of anger. *Psychotherapy*, 23, 629–633. http://dx.doi.org/10.1037/h0085667

Freedman, S. R., & Enright, R. D. (1996). Forgiveness as an intervention goal with incest survivors. *Journal of Consulting and Clinical Psychology*, 64(5), 983–992. http://dx.doi.org/10.1037/0022-006X.64.5.983

Gambaro, M. E., Enright, R. D., Baskin, T. A., & Klatt, J. (2008). Can school-based forgiveness counseling improve conduct and academic achievement in academically at-risk adolescents? *Journal of Research in Education*, 18, 16–27.

Hansen, M. J., Enright. R. D., Baskin, T. W., & Klatt, J. (2009). A palliative care intervention in forgiveness therapy for elderly terminally-ill cancer patients. *Journal of Palliative Care*, 25, 51–60. PMid: 19445342

Holter, A. C., Magnuson, C., Knutson, C., Knutson Enright, J. A., & Enright, R. D. (2008). The forgiving child: The impact of forgiveness education on excessive anger for elementary-aged children in Milwaukee's central city. *Journal of Research in Education*, 18, 82–93.

Lin, W. F., Mack, D., Enright, R. D., Krahn, D., & Baskin, T. (2004). Effects of forgiveness therapy on anger, mood, and vulnerability to substance use among inpatient substance-dependent clients. *Jour-

nal of Consulting and Clinical Psychology, 72(6), 1114–1121. http://dx.doi.org/10.1037/0022-006X.72.6.1114; PMid:15612857

Park, J. H., Enright, R. D., Essex, M. J., Zahn-Waxler, C., & Klatt, J. S. (2013). Forgiveness intervention for female South Korean adolescent aggressive victims. *Journal of Applied Developmental Psychology*, 20, 393–402. http://dx.doi.org/10.1016/j.appdev.2013.06.001

Reed, G., & Enright, R. D. (2006). The effects of forgiveness therapy on depression, anxiety, and post-traumatic stress for women after spousal emotional abuse. *Journal of Consulting and Clinical Psychology*, 74, 920–929. http://dx.doi.org/10.1037/0022-006X. 74.5. 920; PMid:17032096

Ricciardi, E., Rota, G., Sani, L., Gentili, C., Gaglianese, A., Guazzelli, M., & Petrini, P. (2013). How the brain heals emotional wounds: The functional neuroanatomy of forgiveness. *Frontiers in Human Neuroscience*, 7, article 839, 1–9 (quotation is from page 1). doi: 10.3389/fnhum.2013.00839

Waltman, M. A., Russell, D. C., Coyle, C. T., Enright, R. D., Holter, A. C., & Swoboda, C. (2009). The effects of a forgiveness intervention on patients with coronary artery disease. *Psychology and Health*, 24, 11–27. http://dx.doi.org/10.1080/08870440801975127; PMid: 20186637

Wilder, T. (1938/1957). *Our town: A play in three acts*. New York: Harper & Row.

Vitz, P. C., & Meade, J. (2011). Self-forgiveness in psychology and psychotherapy: A critique. *Journal of Religion and Health*, 50, 248–259. doi: 10.1007/s10943-010-343-x.

Index